Successful Strategic Planning: Case Studies

Douglas W. Steeples, *Editor*
University of Southern Colorado

NEW DIRECTIONS FOR HIGHER EDUCATION

MARTIN KRAMER, *Editor-in-Chief*
University of California, Berkeley

Number 64, Winter 1988

Paperback sourcebooks in
The Jossey-Bass Higher Education Series

Jossey-Bass Inc., Publishers
San Francisco • London

Douglas W. Steeples (ed.).
Successful Strategic Planning: Case Studies.
New Directions for Higher Education, no. 64.
Volume XVI, number 4.
San Francisco: Jossey-Bass, 1988.

New Directions for Higher Education
Martin Kramer, *Editor-in-Chief*

New Directions for Higher Education is published quarterly
by Jossey-Bass Inc., Publishers (publication number USPS
990-880). *New Directions* is numbered sequentially—please
order extra copies by sequential number. The volume and issue
numbers above are included for the convenience of libraries.
Second-class postage paid at San Francisco, California, and at
additional mailing offices. POSTMASTER: Send address changes
to Jossey-Bass Inc., Publishers, 350 Sansome Street, San Francisco,
California 94104.

Editorial correspondence should be sent to the Editor-in-Chief,
Martin Kramer, 2807 Shasta Road, Berkeley, California 94708.

Library of Congress Catalog Card Number LC 85-644752

International Standard Serial Number ISSN 0271-0560

International Standard Book Number ISBN 1-55542-887-8

Cover art by WILLI BAUM

Manufactured in the United States of America. Printed on acid-free paper.

Ordering Information

The paperback sourcebooks listed below are published quarterly and can be ordered either by subscription or single copy.

Subscriptions cost $52.00 per year for institutions, agencies, and libraries. Individuals can subscribe at the special rate of $39.00 per year *if payment is by personal check.* (Note that the full rate of $52.00 applies if payment is by institutional check, even if the subscription is designated for an individual.) Standing orders are accepted.

Single copies are available at $12.95 when payment accompanies order. (California, New Jersey, New York, and Washington, D.C., residents please include appropriate sales tax.) For billed orders, cost per copy is $12.95 plus postage and handling.

Substantial discounts are offered to organizations and individuals wishing to purchase bulk quantities of Jossey-Bass sourcebooks. Please inquire.

Please note that these prices are for the calendar year 1988 and are subject to change without notice. Also, some titles may be out of print and therefore not available for sale.

To ensure correct and prompt delivery, all orders must give either the *name of an individual* or an *official purchase order number.* Please submit your order as follows:

Subscriptions: specify series and year subscription is to begin.
Single Copies: specify sourcebook code (such as, HE1) and first two words of title.

Mail orders for United States and Possessions, Australia, New Zealand, Canada, Latin America, and Japan to:
Jossey-Bass Inc., Publishers
350 Sansome Street
San Francisco, California 94104

Mail orders for all other parts of the world to:
Jossey-Bass Limited
28 Banner Street
London EC1Y 8QE

New Directions for Higher Education Series
Martin Kramer, *Editor-in-Chief*

Contents

Editor's Notes

Samuel Johnson once remarked of an acquaintance, who, when he was facing imminent execution, had become an impressively prolific and articulate writer of letters of appeal, that it concentrated one's mind wonderfully to know that one was to be hanged within twenty-four hours. Almost the same can be said for an important segment of American higher education over the last decade or so. A newly volatile and competitive era, brought on by profound demographic, social, economic, and political changes, has confronted academic administrators with a battery of threats, challenges, and opportunities requiring thoughtful responses. Never before has the task of shaping the futures of their institutions demanded such concentration, imagination, and resourcefulness.

The publication of Lewis B. Mayhew's (1979) *Surviving the Eighties* heralded the new era. Mayhew prophesied sharp competition to maintain enrollments, as the annual classes of eighteen-year-olds would shrink throughout the 1980s. Colleges and universities would have to become shrewd marketers, skilled in modern management practices, adept at enrollment management, and sophisticated in their understanding of the uses and limitations of academic program modification. Other writers forecast the demise of as many as 400 colleges by the early 1990s, a prediction made credible by the fact that 141 private institutions had failed to survive the 1970s.

George Keller's (1983) *Academic Strategy* proposed a management approach attuned to the requirements of the times; more than any other single work, it directed the attention of academics to the concept of strategic planning. Unlike the older approach of long-range planning, which typically projected model institutional futures based on linear extrapolations from the past, strategic planning is essentially action-oriented. Although strategic planning also addresses longer-term goals, it emphasizes actions to be taken in the shorter term, often a year to eighteen months. It is fundamentally a systematic method based on an assessment of the institution's internal strengths and weaknesses and the threats and opportunities existing in the external environment—a method that allows institutions to make decisions for action about mission, goals, markets, priorities, and programs. It promises adaptive management.

This sourcebook is about successful strategic planning. It is grounded in practice and experience, rather than theory and research. It presents firsthand accounts of effective strategic planning, as conducted by practitioners who used that approach as a potent device for shaping the futures of their colleges and universities. The contributors are all either current or former presidents, as well as prime movers in the accounts that they provide. As reports of success, the accounts furnish compelling examples of the resourcefulness and resiliency of American higher education in challenging times, and they offer ideas that may be widely applied by institutions seeking to reply creatively to current threats and opportunities.

Robert Shirley, in Chapter One, offers a conceptual introduction to strategic planning. A strategic effort begins with the design of a strategic vision, which Shirley holds to be the highest function of presidential leadership. Defining an institution's basic mission and its target audiences, determining the desired program mix and the institution's comparative market advantage, and specifying the actions required to achieve goals are all part of creating a strategic vision. Matching internal strengths to opportunities lying in the external environment is crucial in conceiving a strategy. The plan must then be put into operation, which involves the completion of congruent plans in operating units or departments. The chapter concludes with a statement of the benefits and the pitfalls of strategic planning.

In Chapter Two, Robert Lisensky establishes the importance of integrating planning with assessment and with institutional control systems. Continuing assessment permits timely revision of goals as experience recommends. Careful management of control systems articulates operations with plans. The most important control system is budgeting, which can prioritize allocation of resources in line with planning goals. The information system, reward system, and procedures for meshing unit plans with the overall plan are also vital control devices. Strong presidential leadership, efforts to build consensus as to goals, and a due respect for the prevailing institutional culture also contribute to successful strategic efforts.

David Brown, in Chapter Three, describes the University of North Carolina at Asheville (UNCA), and he, too, stresses the importance of visionary leadership while showing that a strategic plan is always in process, always under revision as circumstances unfold. A temporarily favorable climate in the state legislature that allowed major campus construction enabled a new campus master site plan to function as a planning catalyst at UNCA. Other important elements in the strategic effort included the designation of program "thrust areas" to be supported with venture funding, imaginative measures to improve the university's service to its region, undertakings to broaden the base of support for the institution, and steps to elevate and broaden its aspirations.

In Chapter Four, Richard Morrill shows how the central elements of the identity of Centre College of Kentucky helped frame a planning venture that grew through two years of research and a broadly participatory process of goal definition. Small size, a commitment to liberal learning in a coeducational and residential setting, and pride in a heritage of academic rigor informed the development of a vision of Centre as a national model for institutions of its size and type. Completion of a list of measurable goals and of a program for assessing progress contributed to a period of striking institutional advancement.

At the University of Louisville, as Donald Swain shows in Chapter Five, vigorous presidential leadership worked with a carefully defined faculty advisory role to create a design for institutional progress. The plan aimed to improve overall quality, increase the emphasis on research, stress and take advantage of an urban mission, provide for speedy adaptation to change, enhance management effectiveness, strengthen bonds with the surrounding community, and heighten the university's standing. The creation of congruent unit operating plans completed the strategic plan.

Ed Roach, in Chapter Six, explains how West Texas State University (WTSU) effectively replied to shrinking state appropriations, calls for mission differentiation among the public institutions of Texas, and a new accreditation renewal requirement for institutional planning. Proceeding very much as Robert Shirley outlined in the opening chapter, WTSU achieved structural reorganization for greater efficiency; a scheme of academic prioritization governing decisions to enhance, maintain, reduce, or in some instances eliminate programs; and the development of a facilities and site plan that emphasized careful stewardship in managing public resources, set an example for the state, and promised to meet foreseeable needs into the next century. Significant improvements in external support, enrollment and student quality, and many aspects of operations followed.

In Chapter Seven, I describe how Westminster College of Salt Lake City recovered from the prospect of imminent closure, in the face of virtual bankruptcy, to unprecedented vigor through determined applications of a strategy that evolved over a period of several years. An outside consultant, engaged after the college entered financial exigency in 1979, provided the basic strategic design. Tenacious administrative leadership employed a faculty task force to revise and then win faculty acceptance and implementation of a changed mission statement, a modified calendar, a reshaped general education program, and, finally, a retrenchment that followed a review and prioritization of academic offerings. Later, when the threat of closure necessitated bold measures conceived in secrecy, faculty loyalty and support were crucial to the success of a dramatic reorganization, program realignment, and marketing effort that accompanied a final retrenchment. More clearly than in any other case in this sourcebook, urgent threats provided the impetus for strategic planning at Westminster.

Edward Foote, in Chapter Eight, recounts the ongoing evolution of the planning process at the University of Miami. Planners at Miami continuously revise goals as conditions change but within the limits

4

imposed by a broad set of guidelines. These standards stress doing well all that is attempted, the importance to a university of faculty research, the potential for long life of a contemplated initiative, the capacity for building synergistically on existing strengths, critical-mass requirements, expense, and appropriateness of objectives. Other constants include regard for the university's mission and consideration of the special characteristics and obligations inherent in its environment, program priorities, goals, action plans, and resource needs. Over a period of five years, the planning process has resulted in major gains for the institution, creatively balancing the centrifugal individual aspirations of students and faculty with the centripetal forces that keep the institution intact. Presidential vision and proposals have played a singular role throughout.

Richard Cyert's review, in Chapter Nine, of planning at Carnegie Mellon University concludes the case histories. Like the other authors, Cyert stresses the importance of seeking a distinctive market advantage or niche that places the institution in a unique position. At Carnegie Mellon, the objective is to produce focused departments whose strengths buttress a mission in which technical education is central. Since this university, like most American institutions of higher education, is decentralized in character, collaboration between the president and the faculty is imperative, as is flexibility in adapting goals to changing conditions.

The final chapter offers concluding observations. It identifies the characteristics common to these examples of successful strategic planning. In doing so, it comments on the crucial elements of the planning process and the uses of strategic planning. The connection between strategic planning and action receives special attention. Closing remarks consider the limits of strategic planning, the constraints that confine its employment, and the promise that it holds.

Douglas W. Steeples
Editor

References

Keller, G. *Academic Strategy: The Management Revolution in Higher Education.* Baltimore, Md.: Johns Hopkins University Press, 1983.
Mayhew, L. B. *Surviving the Eighties: Strategies and Procedures for Solving Fiscal and Enrollment Problems.* San Francisco: Jossey-Bass, 1979.

Douglas W. Steeples is dean of the College of Liberal and Fine Arts at the University of Southern Colorado and has served as executive vice-president and academic dean at Westminster College, Utah.

*Strategic planning is a process that articulates institutional
mission, weighs external opportunities and threats, gauges
internal strengths and weaknesses, and determines appropriate
action.*

Strategic Planning:
An Overview

Robert C. Shirley

More and more colleges and universities are recognizing the need to plan
strategically—that is, the need to articulate clearly a vision for the future
and to specify the means by which the vision is to be realized. This
vision should seek to develop the optimal relationship between institutional capabilities and values, on the one hand, and environmental needs
and opportunities, on the other. The diversity of experiences reported in
this sourcebook shows that institutions differ dramatically in how they
go about planning and creating their desired futures. All successful strategic planning efforts, however, have two results in common: clarity of
purpose and direction, and the specification of action steps required to
accomplish the overall purpose. The major goal of the planning process
itself is to achieve clarity of purpose and vision for the institution as a
whole and for its component parts.

This chapter presents a concept of planning that applies to all types
of colleges and universities and that can be used both to create and to
evaluate an institutional plan. Strategic planning as it applies to an
entire institution will receive primary attention, with unit-level planning
within an institution receiving only secondary consideration.

D. W. Steeples (ed.). *Successful Strategic Planning: Case Studies.*
New Directions for Higher Education, no. 64. San Francisco: Jossey-Bass, Winter 1988.

Developing a Strategic Vision

Defining a vision that is inspiring to faculty, staff, students, and the external community is the highest function of presidential leadership. After securing appropriate advice and encouraging adequate discussion within the college or university and after consulting with leaders of the wider community, the chief executive officer is responsible for articulating and communicating the vision. The acid test of presidential leadership is the extent to which the vision both serves as the unifying force for individual and group behavior within the institution and generates strong support in the external community.

In order for the vision to be specific and compelling, it must reflect decisions that have been made about the critical developmental paths for the college or university. A strategic vision unites decisions in five major areas: institutional mission, target audiences, program offerings and priorities, comparative advantage, and the key objectives to be pursued. A brief discussion of each of these follows.

Basic Mission. Defining the mission of the institution is the first and most fundamental component of the overall institutional plan. The purpose of a mission statement is to set out the nature, shape, and character of the institution. Several issues must be addressed and resolved in the course of fixing institutional mission:

Fundamental Purposes and Overall Goals. What is the basic reason for the existence of the college or university? This is an abstract but essential element of the overall plan. Included here should be the broad goals that the institution seeks to accomplish on behalf of students and society.

Special Characteristics. What is the unique character of the institution? Uniqueness may be derived from geographic location, legislative mandate, religious ties, or other special campus characteristics.

Constituencies to Be Served. What constituencies are to be served, and what are the institution's general obligations to each? All relevant constituencies should be noted, including students, employers, alumni, and others with a special stake in the institution.

Geographic Service Area. What are the physical boundaries of the institution's activities? Whether a college or university is national, regional, state, or purely local in nature depends on many variables, but the primary focus of service needs to be stated as clearly as possible.

Major Emphases and Commitments. What relative emphasis does the institution place on teaching, research, and service? This element addresses selectivity in the admission of students and the importance, if any, of competitive student achievement. It delimits the roles of graduate and undergraduate education, liberal education and career preparation, the classical disciplines and the professional fields, and cocurricular experiences and breadth as opposed to specialization. Specificity is important here in order to communicate the values of the institution in each of these vital areas.

Academic Freedom and Corollary Obligations. What is the institution's position concerning academic freedom, and what is the philosophical basis for that position? Also to be included here are the obligations that accompany the responsible exercise of academic freedom.

Form of Governance and Management. What decision-making roles are played by the institution's administration, faculty, students, governing board, statewide commissions, and other agencies? The reigning conception of shared governance and the respective roles of major participants in shaping decisions should be made clear here.

Community and Civic Obligations. What is the institution's role in the wider community, and does that role take the form of active leadership or of a more passive citizenship? Clarification of position on the leadership-citizenship continuum is important in order to determine appropriate institutional actions with regard to the surrounding community.

The mission statement proclaims the guiding vision and aspirations of the institution. It needs to be inspiring and to set forth goals that are both worthy and at a level of accomplishment appropriate for faculty, staff, and students. It must avoid the most common failing of such pieces—vagueness that, in claiming too much, really claims nothing—and be specific, communicating guiding principles for behavior to all members of the enterprise.

Target Audiences. Colleges and universities serve a number of audiences. Among these are students, employers, the local community, "friends" of the institution, and others. The precise definition of target audiences requires the resolution of four critical problems.

The first task is to determine which fundamental needs the institution aims to address. The institution must consider the needs characteristic of each constituency to be served. For example, the institution should conduct research to discover why students do and do not enroll, in order to determine which student needs are currently being served and which are not. The findings will enable planners to decide whether or not the student needs that are to be served in the future should differ dramatically from those that are currently being addressed. The needs in question may be academic, career, social, physical, or emotional in character. Similar research should be conducted to assess the needs of each target audience.

The next step is to fix the number of students to be served. Planners must determine the optimum size of the college or university—financially, physically, and educationally. A precise goal is not necessary, but an appropriate range of numbers for the desired size of the student population should be identified.

The third task is to identify the desired target mix of intellectual interests, as indicated by the distribution of students among different majors. The problem here is one of intellectual balance, of ensuring the presence in desirable proportions of students possessing intellectual interests appropriate to the mission of the college or university. The current popularity of business administration as a major is forcing many institutions to decide whether or not to limit the number of students pursuing business degrees in order to maintain the desired intellectual ambiance. Without serious attention to this and similar issues of intellectual mix, changing student preferences may work at cross-purposes with institutional mission.

Finally, planners must consider the appropriate demographic mix on campus. It is vital that the distributions of students' geographic origins, ages, ability levels, resident or commuter statuses, and ethnic backgrounds, as well as the male to female ratio, help to maintain the institution's intended learning and living environment.

Program Mix. Definition of the institution's optimal program mix is a strategic decision of great importance. Three major issues must be dealt with: specification of program offerings, determination of the priorities among these programs, and fixing of the focal points for new program development over an extended time period. Both internal and external factors must be considered in making these decisions. Internally, faculty capabilities, the centrality of various programs to the mission of the institution, the availability of library resources, the quantity and quality of facilities and equipment available to support various programs, and cost must be taken into account. Externally, demand by students, needs of employers, resources available in the surrounding area, competing programs at other institutions, and degree of community impact must be assessed. These elements must be weighed with care before one makes strategic judgments about program offerings, priorities, and developmental emphases for the future.

Decisions about program offerings and priorities are the most crucial and most sensitive components in a strategic planning effort. They are at the heart of a college's or university's identity. They can involve volatile staffing and other personnel issues. Many institutions persist in offering an excessive number of programs, thereby diminishing the level of quality that can be achieved. An effective strategic planning effort must place primary emphasis on the question of program mix if institutional energies and resources are to be used most productively.

Comparative Advantage. Growing competition for students makes it increasingly important for a college or university to consider how it can gain a comparative advantage over other institutions through the development of a strategic vision for the future. It is competition in the healthiest sense when institutions seek to develop unique positions within the wider higher education environment. The differentiation of mission or programs can result in a strategic advantage. Enhancements in the physical appearance of the campus or in extracurricular opportunities, attractive adjustments in the academic calendar, improved services to students, or similar measures, may offer operational advantages as well. Regardless of how one attempts to differentiate the institution, the notion of strategic positioning to capitalize on a particular market niche enjoys growing popularity in higher education. Society also benefits from the resulting differentiation of institutions, as a broader array of educational choices and experiences becomes available to students.

Key Objectives. The final set of decisions made in shaping most strategic visions is the identification of the key objectives, of the principal action steps needed to move a college or university from the existing to the desired state of affairs. The major actions required to move from the present to the planned condition, once an institution has articulated its mission, target audiences, program mix, and intended comparative advantages, are termed "objectives" in the language of strategic planning. Objectives should be limited in number (to perhaps ten or so) to permit the most effective focusing of institutional energy. For the same reason, they should also concentrate on substance, not form.

Action steps typically center on human resources, financial resources, physical resources, enrollment, image, instructional programs, research, community service, and organizational structure and climate. Measures taken in these areas propel the campus toward realization of its strategic vision.

Strategic Versus Operational Decisions

Strategic decisions, in the five realms discussed above, differ from operational, or implementation, decisions. Strategic planning as a process begins by defining the vision for the institution; it results in implementation decisions, which relate the vision to day-to-day operations. Operational plans are thus required to channel institutional activities, within the boundaries of the vision, in the domains of finances, facilities, enrollment, human resources, and organization. These operational plans are institutionwide and set the general parameters for unit-level strategic planning.

Once the strategic vision and operational plans are in place, then each academic and administrative unit on campus can devise its own strategic profile for the future, consistent with the comprehensive college or university design. Coherence and consistency of direction are the criteria for unit-level plans, not mindless conformity. Entrepreneurial variations often occur and, indeed, should be encouraged. At the same time, to accomplish the mission and priorities articulated in the comprehensive plan, a broad and coordinated range of activities at the unit level is necessary in order to focus the institution's efforts.

Analyses Essential to Sound Planning Decisions

The strategic, operational, and unit-level decisions represent the destination points in any effective strategic planning venture. If these decisions are to be informed and judicious, they must be supported by analyses of relevant information. Typically, three types of analyses must participate in a strategic planning enterprise: measurement of external opportunities, threats, and constraints; assessment of institutional strengths and weaknesses; and analysis of the group and personal values held by organization members. A common instrument for such analyses is the position paper.

External Environment. The measurement of external opportunities, threats, and constraints should identify both the positive and the negative aspects of the outside environment. Chief among the factors to be weighed are economic, demographic, political, legal, technological, and social conditions and changes. To a certain extent, these affect all colleges and universities. At the same time, there are important local differences, and institutions themselves vary significantly in how they experience these influences. Thus it is essential that the analytical efforts be geared toward helping to resolve the issues related to mission, target audiences, program mix, comparative advantage, and objectives. Every position paper prepared concerning a major external influence should identify the specific ramifications for strategic decision making.

External analyses should be crisp and concise, with no more than a paragraph or two devoted to discussion of a particular factor. Moreover, the number of factors considered as relevant to strategic decision making should be limited to no more than twenty-five or thirty. It is essential to concentrate attention on the most critical external influences on a college's or a university's future.

Institutional Strengths and Weaknesses. The assessment of internal strengths and weaknesses usually centers on six areas: human capital, financial resources, quality of facilities, program, image, and the character of the organization. The purpose of this assessment is to ascertain specifically what an institution can and what it cannot do. As in the case of external factors, the implications of the findings for strategic decision making should be specifically identified. The objectives established for the future are often aimed at correcting the serious weaknesses discovered in this analysis. At the same time, the institution can capitalize on existing advantages by defining objectives that employ its strengths.

Role of Values. The analysis of personal values as a component in decision making has not received enough attention in the literature or the practice of planning. Personal values, which include one's "conception of the desirable," are critical determinants of personal and group responses to the overall strategic plan. Among other things, values define what groups and individuals want to do as the institution moves through time. Like it or not, values will intrude in the decision-making process, as planners frame strategies for the future. For these reasons, and particularly because of the need to secure commitment to the strategic vision, personal and group preferences for alternative missions, priorities, target audiences, and objectives should be given appropriate weight as a campus community proceeds toward planning decisions.

Matching Findings. The crucial step in the analysis of external trends, institutional strengths and weaknesses, and relevant personal values is the matching of congruent findings. For example, the external analysis may reveal significant opportunities for which there are insufficient institutional capabilities. There might also be points of institutional strength that no longer match external trends. Or there could be a match of institutional strengths with external opportunities, while the values of key individuals or groups point toward an alternative course for the college or university. These three examples of mismatch emphasize the need to defer final strategic decisions until the findings from each of the three analytical areas have been examined in relation to one another. The matching process is the critical transitional step between the analysis of key factors and the formulation of a strategic vision for the future.

Benefits of Planning

Strategic planning offers five primary benefits. The first benefit derives from the communication of a strategic vision. It is true that visions take different forms and represent varying degrees of sophistication. What is important is that the vision for a particular institution be clear and inspiring to organizational members and to external constituents. In order to be inspiring, the vision must present appropriate challenges of a high order; otherwise, the actions proposed appear to be routine and unworthy of full loyalty and effort. The vision must also represent a realistic level of aspiration for the campus and its constituents. If error is unavoidable, it is best to err on the side of aspiration in order to hold out appropriate challenges. The benefit deriving from the communication of a soundly conceived strategic vision is that such a vision may win a commitment from both internal and external constituents to accomplish shared, inspiring goals.

The second major benefit of planning is the increase in external support that normally follows a clear articulation of vision. Expanded support takes many forms, of which one of the most common is enlarged financial contributions to the institution from individuals, foundations, and granting agencies of various types. Benefactors are becoming more sophisticated in their giving; consequently, they seek assurance that their gifts are being used wisely and are indeed furthering the well-being of the college or university. One of the best ways to persuade them that their gifts will "make a difference" is to present a coherent vision for the future. Put another way, an institution should put its own house in order and demonstrate wise use of available resources before undertaking active solicitation of new contributors. As a rule, all forms of outside support tend to grow when an institution has framed a specific, clear direction for the future.

The third key benefit of planning arises from the increased certainty it brings to the lives of organizational members. Few things are more deleterious to organizational and individual well-being than lack of certainty about goals, priorities, and the direction of future development. Strategic planning brings certainty of intent to the life of the institution, although it does not necessarily guarantee a specific course of events. Assurance about intent, however, brings confidence that future actions, whatever their concrete form, will be consistent with the institution's vision.

The fourth chief benefit of planning is that it provides a context for resource allocation and reallocation on campus. Too often, budgets are shaped on the basis of short-term, even political considerations, without reference to the institution's longer-term mission and priorities. The strategic plan greatly eases the task of resource management. When specific decisions about program mix exist, for example, it will be clear which programs are to receive enhanced and which are to receive the same or lesser support over the next several years. Linking budgeting with planning then becomes a test of will rather than of technique. Adherence to the plan can thus reduce significantly the roles of politics and personal influence in the budgeting process.

The final primary benefit of planning is that it improves the institution's image. The college or university can become known as "a place with a future" precisely because it has envisioned the future that it is working to create for itself. This development can lead, in turn, to a reputation for innovation and progressive thinking that is attractive to potential students and benefactors.

Common Pitfalls in Planning

There are pitfalls as well as benefits associated with strategic planning. The most serious failing of most planning efforts is an inability to achieve closure on major issues. Strategic planning must be strongly decision-oriented if it is to succeed. When the hard issues are avoided, planning efforts quickly lose credibility; thus, a strong commitment to make decisions must precede the planning process. In other words, there must be a prior commitment to articulate the mission, define the target audiences, identify program offerings and priorities, determine a comparative advantage, and state key objectives for the future. This commitment is essential to the future health of the campus as well as to the morale of the participants in planning.

Another common pitfall is an overemphasis on data collection and analysis. The tendency to quantify inherently qualitative phenomena should be avoided. Strategic decision making involves many uncertainties, and the inclination to search unceasingly for the elusive "perfect answer" slows too many planning efforts.

There is also the danger that planning can become too "bureaucratized." Use of standardized forms and excessive paperwork are the two primary indicators of this condition. The employment of forms should be minimized, and page limits should be set for position papers and other written elements in the process. It is also important to avoid much of the planning jargon that has appeared in the recent literature in order to maintain credibility with the faculty.

A further planning error is failure to gain adequate campuswide participation. Even when a democratic, grass-roots process selects a planning group, there is a tendency for the group to become isolated from colleagues and peers. Planning groups should energetically encourage the involvement of their colleagues. Open hearings, newsletters, active solicitation of ideas—these and other strategies should be employed to create a sense of identification with and ownership of the planning process throughout the campus community.

Planners may also err by neglecting to keep significant external constituents informed of progress, particularly constituents who may hold ultimate authority over the affairs of the institution. The governing board should receive periodic planning process reports, as should any relevant statewide coordinating commission. Surprises should be kept to a minimum, externally as well as internally.

An institution must follow through on its strategic planning with appropriate implementation strategies. Some excellent institutional plans have fallen far short of their promise during the implementation stage. Properly overseeing the implementation of plans requires a strong commitment from the president and the other top officers, but it also requires establishing an organizational mechanism to monitor progress. Many planning groups are now serving as standing committees of the institution and are charged with the implementation, as well as the formulation, of strategic plans.

The final major trap into which planners can fall is timidity. The strategic plan established for a college or a university must be stimulating and reach for a higher level of institutional attainment in the future. Many plans, in contrast, merely project existing activities into the future in linear fashion. It is essential to search for the new, the unusual, and the creative, as well as to preserve and improve the central, if the obligations of institutions of higher learning are to be met. And, once the bold stroke has been made, it must be publicized and given wide attention throughout the campus and the surrounding community. Employed with discipline, determination, and courage, strategic planning offers colleges and universities a powerful means of shaping their futures in a rapidly changing environment.

Robert C. Shirley is president of the University of Southern Colorado.

*In today's volatile environment, the coordination of planning
with assessment and with budgeting is essential to the good
health of a college or university.*

Integrating the Control Systems

Robert P. Lisensky

"Happy families are all alike; every unhappy family is unhappy in its
own way" (Tolstoy [1875–1877] 1970, p. 1). We could also say that healthy
colleges and universities are alike, in that they share certain characteristics
that are missing or are imperfectly developed in their unhealthy counter-
parts. Among the most important of these characteristics are: a clearly
articulated and widely shared vision of what the institution wants to
accomplish; a plan with which to move the institution where it needs to
go; a means for collecting and using information for self-assessment; and
a willingness to engage in self-corrective action.

The first characteristic of a healthy institution of higher education is
that it has developed a mission statement that articulates its unique
strengths, the goals that it wishes to achieve, and the values that will
govern program assessment and the distribution of resources. A second
characteristic is a planning process that employs wide participation and
that is generally understood and supported by the campus community.
Evaluation, or assessment, is a vital part of this process. Evaluation must
discover what works and why. It must determine what is not working
and what should be done about it. Institutions need to evaluate their
activity on a continuing basis and fine-tune their plans wherever assessment recommends.

D. W. Steeples (ed.). *Successful Strategic Planning: Case Studies.*
New Directions for Higher Education, no. 64. San Francisco: Jossey-Bass, Winter 1988.

In higher education, planning, assessment, and budgeting have often developed as separate, unrelated procedures. Although budgeting should form the practical link between planning and assessment, it has often functioned as an end in itself. Too frequently, it has depended on a linear projection of past spending practices into the future, rather than on a sharply defined set of institutional priorities that might reshape expenditures.

It is the thesis of this chapter that linking planning, assessment, and budgeting is vital to the well-being of any college or university. Planning and assessment enable an institution to make decisions about day-to-day activities and future goals, revising them as experience suggests. Resource allocation is what converts the decisions and goals into actions.

Linking Planning, Assessment, Budgeting

In practical terms, integrating planning, assessment, and budgeting may not be easy. Administrators and faculty members are often frustrated and disappointed by their experiences, as the following comments from participants in planning workshops indicate:

- "Our planning process is static. We gave all of our energies to the development of mission and goal statements and have had little follow-up."
- "We have confused the entire institution by tying strategic planning to operational planning and annual budgeting."
- "Department heads and program directors do not understand how their program objectives tie into institutional goals and objectives."
- "We have not taken time to determine what data is [sic] important for the planning process and, therefore, have little idea what additional data is needed."

Strategic Planning as the Instrument of Integration. Daniel H. Gray (1986) has suggested one way to coordinate planning, assessment, and budgeting: "*Strategic management* . . . regards planning as an instrument *around which* all other control systems—budgeting, information, compensation, organization—can be integrated" (p. 89). Most of the problems that colleges and universities have experienced in the planning, assessment, and budgeting processes have stemmed from the fact that planning has not been used as the instrument of integration.

To do so, planners must possess a firm grasp of existing problems. When National Center for Higher Education Management Systems (NCHEMS) staff members work with colleges and universities, we often find that the areas that have received the most attention, such as broad constituency participation, administrative commitment, and analysis of internal and external environments, are not really as critical as some other, often unrecognized, problems.

Confusing Operational with Strategic Planning. One such problem has to do with the inability to distinguish between "operational" and "strategic" planning. Operational planning relies on the individual units—for example, the academic departments or divisions within a college and the colleges or schools within a university—to gather and interpret information and to develop their own operating plans. This practice assumes that the current array of separate operating units is adequate. As a result, the guiding questions then become "How much should be added?" or "How much should be cut?" within each unit rather than "What should we be doing?" and "Which priorities should control the distribution of resources?" The viewpoint that governs is local, rather than institutional.

Two criticisms are frequently directed at operational planning. The first is that it has a tendency to be self-centered and to ignore the external environment. This fault can be corrected if each functional unit enjoys access to appropriate data about the external environment. The second is that operational planning usually accepts "what is" as what ought to be and accordingly projects in linear fashion from the present into the future. In reply to these criticisms, we must note that the operational approach and its outcomes are useful in many ways. Each unit, after all, has its own genuine concerns that can be addressed most effectively at the local level.

At the same time, it is important that an institution not rely solely on planning at the unit level as a means to shape its future. Colleges and universities need both operational and strategic planning. Both kinds of planning work incrementally, and each needs to possess access to data about the external environment. What, then, is the difference between them? The difference is the unit of analysis. For strategic planning, the unit of analysis is the entire institution. While units need to identify their specific goals, the central administration must determine the strategic issues for the entire institution; this is the process called strategic planning. When top administrators do not engage in this process, it is extremely difficult, if not impossible, for effective planning to occur.

Compartmentalizing Management Functions. Another problem might be termed the "compartmentalization syndrome," where planning is carried out without relation to other management activities. Various control systems—for example, information, reward, and budget, in addition to planning—operate as if they were independent enterprises.

Each of these areas of control holds tremendous potential for knitting an institution together if it functions in concert with the others. For instance, a college or university must maintain an information system geared to gathering and analyzing certain critical sets of data if it is to plan effectively. Developing such a system requires an understanding of what constitutes strategic planning information and how to use it. However, most information systems in colleges and universities deal simply with the separate functions of the institution, such as admissions, registration, payroll, and so on. The premium is placed on accuracy and detail with respect to the day-to-day activities of individual offices. What is often missing is a comprehensive picture of the status and activities of the entire institution in its charging demographic, social, economic, and political environments.

Identifying the Information Needed for Planning. A third problem, closely related to the last, is the lack of an adequate information base that would allow the integration of planning, assessment, and budget. An early step in the planning process, then, is the identification of what data the institution has already collected, who controls this information, and how to integrate it with other, new information that may be required for a comprehensive understanding. Strategic planning will employ operational data, and it will also need trend data, much of the latter drawn from outside the institution, documenting significant changes that have occurred over a considerable period of time. The result must be a body of information that helps the institution focus on critical issues and communicate its priorities. By providing the campus with the necessary information, the planners can help set the stage for debate.

Using the Budget as the Key Control System

The budget is the crucial control system, so it is critically important that the budget be integrated into the planning process. Resource allocation is one of the most powerful of administration's management tools. Spending authorizations provide incentives for change in desired directions. They are the mechanism for translating plans into action, for channeling resources toward the accomplishment of goals.

Budgeting, in most colleges and universities, is a process of making incremental adjustments up or down from the previous year's allocation. The funding base is defined in terms of financial precedents rather than in terms of programmatic aims or priorities. In order to link planning with budgeting, administrators must find a method to transcend the annual budget cycle, with its tendency to perpetuate what is rather than to explore and elaborate what ought to be.

Targeting Allocations. One way to connect the budget with planning is to employ special-purpose allocations. With this method, institutions set aside 1 to 2 percent of the operating budget to fund programs developed or identified for emphasis through the planning process. Often this approach is the only means by which to fund institutional change and transcend well-established allocation practices.

Special-purpose allocations also enable a college or university to direct funds to specifically defined objectives. A program funded by means of this device displays three important characteristics: There is a specific time frame for implementation of the project; there is a more detailed description of program objectives than in a typical budget item; and there is, as a result, a greater than usual opportunity to assess outcomes.

Historically, accountability has been perceived in terms of spending funds in accordance with budget line-item authorizations. Special-purpose allocations establish a direct link between performance expectations and budgets. Their use shifts the question from "Did you use resources as budgeted?" to "Did you accomplish your goal?" It holds the advantage of transferring decisions about resource distribution from those responsible for preparing the budget to those responsible for determining and achieving the goals of the institution.

Reviewing Accomplishments. After the first year of strategic planning activity, it is important to assess the effectiveness of specific plans and to evaluate institutional goals, with an eye to making any revisions that experience or altered conditions might indicate. One institution begins a new cycle of the planning process by examining the previous year's priorities and the degree of success with which they were accomplished and by analyzing major deviations from the budget. This practice allows the institution's planning council to monitor performance and identify needed changes in a regular and recurring fashion, and it suggests an important and practical way in which planning, assessment, and budget can be linked.

Coordinating Effort and Building Consensus

It has been suggested that academic institutions have declined, not because of inattention to modern management practices, but because of a loss of a shared system of values. One of the by-products of a successful planning process is the growth on campus of shared institutional values. Successful planning requires that institutional goals be talked out until general agreement has been reached. Thus, a major feature of effectively functioning strategic planning is that faculty and administrators are able to identify and develop the essential spirit of the institution.

Presidential Leadership. Presidential leadership is the crucial element in successful strategic planning. This leadership makes its most important contribution to the planning process by creating and communicating a vision of possible futures for the institution. To work to best advantage, presidential proposals should be general in character; they should encompass such broad areas as the level of academic excellence to be sought, target ranges for student enrollment, approaches to the assessment of student learning outcomes, faculty development, the character of the general education program, and the like. The development of agreed-on campus goals proceeds from vigorous consideration of the president's vision and from the clarification of guiding values that attends this consideration.

Need for Consensus. It is essential to develop campuswide under-standing and acceptance of institutional goals in order to effect necessary change. In general, proposed goals should be consistent with the institu-tional culture and must lie within the constraints of both the internal and the external environment.

Planning Council. Once formulated, intended goals should be shared with a planning council. This body should be composed of representa-tives of the various major institutional constituencies. Faculty involve-ment is of utmost importance; it is one of the mechanisms by which ownership of a plan comes to be shared by an entire campus and, in particular, by which the faculty at large, whose support is essential to the smooth implementation of a plan, come to favor it.

The members of the planning council bear important responsibilities. They need to possess a clear understanding of the institutional goals that the president and central administration propound. They must be skilled listeners as well as effective communicators. They need to be able to gather information and opinions from various units on campus. They should understand that part of their task is to strengthen the shared ideas that emerge in the course of planning council deliberations and in its consultation with units. It is also their job to identify areas where deci-sions and clarification are needed and where it may be necessary to make unpopular choices.

Unit Responses and Plans. After the planning council has reviewed the president's proposals and has selected five or six specific institutional goals, the goals need to be submitted to the campus community so that interested units can devise specific proposals for achieving some of them. It is important at this stage that all of the academic units receive the relevant planning information and enjoy the opportunity to submit ideas. It is also important to recognize that not every unit will wish to do so. Some units will be self- or discipline-preoccupied; some of these same units may well comprise major strengths of the institution. It would be a mistake to compel cooperation from, or to "reform," balky units; coer-cion will not work, and there will be other units that are willing to experiment fruitfully with new programs or initiatives.

Employing an approach that allows for extensive consultation and deliberation, as well as considerable unit autonomy, means, of course, that major change will evolve gradually and with due respect for the existing institutional culture. Such evolutionary change will, in the long run, provide the most secure basis for institutional growth.

When asked to submit proposals to the planning council, the operat-ing units should be informed that their responses are due within a speci-fied period of time. They should also understand that their plans must contain three elements: a statement of the unit's program objectives, a projected timetable for accomplishing these objectives, and a detailed budget plan to support the actions intended. After receiving the unit responses, the planning council must prioritize them and submit them to the president for final approval.

Prioritizing Objectives Through Budgeting

Using a Budget Continuum. One way to integrate planning priorities with institutional action is to employ a budget continuum. The continuum extends from reliance entirely on operating funds, through dependence on grant monies, to provision of no funds. The highest-priority proposals will be supported from the special-purpose allocation created by setting aside 1 to 2 percent of the operating budget. The college or university, meanwhile, will have identified new ideas for which to seek external funding and will be ready to make appropriate decisions if additional revenue becomes available. It will also have become clear that certain areas or ideas will not be funded. In order for the budget continuum to be an effective device, the planning council must review the entire body of proposals within the same time period, rather than sequentially. Prolonged, piecemeal assessment of proposals can result in a loss of perspective, comprehensiveness, and, possibly, fairness.

Employing the Reward System. Administrators also need to consider the rewards available to the programs or persons that contribute to successful change. Higher education is an intensely human enterprise; it follows that the planning process needs to incorporate mechanisms with which to reward those who implement desired changes. At the same time, planners must respect the reward system that has evolved over the years on a particular campus. One way to reward is to provide additional program support monies when desired change occurs.

It is also important *not* to punish the persons or units that have not participated by reducing their levels of budget support. Rewards build morale and cooperation. Punishment nourishes demoralization and opposition.

Conclusion

In summary, a healthy college or university needs a mission statement that identifies its unique strengths and special goals; it needs a continuing cycle of planning and assessment that is linked to action through budgeting and that provides coherence and direction to the entire institution. It also needs an understanding of "strategic management," whereby strategic planning is consciously used as the instrument for integrating all other institutional control systems.

Several critical requirements must be met to provide for these needs:

1. The strategic planning process must be grounded in a specific institution's values.

2. The information system supporting the planning process must be capable of analyzing trend data that are drawn from and characterize the external as well as the internal environment and that document changes that have taken place over a considerable period of time.

3. The various important constituencies of the institution must enjoy the opportunity to share in the planning process.

4. Funding for new programs or initiatives developed as a result of strategic planning should be provided by a special-purpose allocation created by reserving 1 to 2 percent of the current operating budget.

5. The special programs and the planning process itself must be assessed each year in order to monitor progress and possibly to revise goals.

6. A reward system—a supplement to the existing one—must be developed to reward the accomplishment of goals.

The three processes—planning (built on a comprehensive information system), assessing, and budgeting—should form a continuing cycle in the life of a college or university. If the information system is well designed and accurate, if the top administrators provide vision and support, if the planners actively involve their constituents, and if the changes that result respect the organizational culture, then the strategic planning cycle, integrated with campus control systems, can gradually transform an institution of higher education.

References

Gray, D. H. "Uses and Misuses of Strategic Planning." *Harvard Business Review*, 1986, *64* (1), 89–97.

Tolstoy, L. *Anna Karenina.* New York: Norton, 1970. (Originally published in the United States 1875–1877.)

Robert P. Lisensky is president of NCHEMS Management Services, Inc., and has served as president of Willamette University.

The development of a strong program, of a campus master plan, and of broad external support helps ensure the success of strategies that enhance the university's distinctiveness, comparative advantages, and quality.

The University of North Carolina at Asheville

David G. Brown

Meet the University of North Carolina at Asheville (UNCA), where the rewards of strategic planning are blatantly visible. Founded in 1927 and now one of sixteen campuses of the University of North Carolina, the school has added 90 percent to its enrollment since 1980. Vital statistics: mean student scores on the Scholastic Aptitude Test of 933 (fourth highest in the UNC system); 800 beds, 3,000 heads, 2,000 full-time equivalent students; 130 full-time equivalent faculty; $1.5 million endowment; 262 acres one mile from the heart of Asheville in a scenic county of 168,000 people; sponsor of three national journals; 150,000-volume library; required sixteen-hour interdisciplinary study of the humanities using original works; average student twenty-seven years old; long-standing emphasis on liberal arts majors with recent addition of career majors such as management; chancellor, installed in 1984, succeeded predecessor who had served for twenty-one years.

In the last three years, UNCA has doubled its endowment, freshman applications, library, science laboratories, student organizations, and investment in all campus buildings (up from $18 million to $43 million). Research grants, playing fields, and column inches in the local newspaper have tripled. The number of visiting scholars has multiplied more than ten times. New programs include the master's of liberal arts degree,

D. W. Steeples (ed.). *Successful Strategic Planning: Case Studies.*
New Directions for Higher Education, no. 64. San Francisco: Jossey-Bass, Winter 1988.

National Conference on Undergraduate Research, National Board of Visitors, North Carolina Center for Creative Retirement, Western North Carolina Arboretum, the honors program, merit scholarships, parents' weekend, and visitation days.

These dramatic changes are the result of a blend of opportunity and intention. The opportunity was provided by a historically strong faculty and curriculum, a highly respected and effective systemwide leadership, a community eager to support a better university, and the special concern of powerful legislators for "catching up" with new buildings and programs. The opportunity was to grow.

The intention was framed in the strategic plan, which was a blueprint of how to grow, a statement of the general parameters for growth. The intention shaped the growth. This chapter treats the elements, process, and concepts that give UNCA its intention.

Role of Leadership

The growth and implementation of UNCA's strategic plan result from conscious leadership, especially by the University Planning Council (UPC) and the chancellor. While more than twenty different constituencies are influencing the plan, most of these groups look first either to the UPC (a highly respected faculty group that regularly participates in both annual budgeting and long-term planning) or to the chancellor for the proposing and endorsing of any bold new initiatives.

New directions require consistent sponsorship from high places. The foremost responsibility of a leader is to have, to understand, to articulate, and to inspire with zeal a vision of what the university is becoming and to provide the structure for accomplishing it. The vision may be inherited from a predecessor, newly minted by the leader, fashioned by a special commission on mission and scope, even mandated from a governing board—but a vision there must be, and the leadership must believe zealously in its worth. Understanding the vision means knowing its decision-making implications in all settings. Articulating the vision means broadcasting to all other decision makers the relevant decision criteria. Finally, inspiring suggests moving people throughout the organization to expend energy, wisdom, and ingenuity toward achieving the vision.

From visionary leadership with zeal, whether from an individual or from a group such as the University Planning Council, comes the courage to risk for high achievements and the consistency that enables distinctive excellence.

Basic Concepts

A number of procedural concepts underlie UNCA's strategic planning methodology.

Meander Toward a Dream. A strategic plan is always "under construction." Details are forever being added. Before all details are specified, the plan is revised. There is never a "Final Planning Document," with i's dotted and t's crossed. The plan is more a sense of direction than a detailed itinerary. The path to the dream is not a straight line with no misadventures; rather, it winds and meanders in the general direction that the strategic plan sets.

Because strategic plans are partial or incomplete, the university can focus first on those elements of the dream that all important constituencies share and can leave the disputed aspects to later discussions and decisions. At UNCA, for example, we are stressing that all undergraduate curricula will contain a major component of liberal arts. As yet unspecified is whether or not we may eventually seek American Assembly of Collegiate Schools of Business accreditation for our management program.

Build on Strengths. By first being made stronger, the strong will be able to strengthen the weak. Directly strengthening weak programs rarely works, does little for the strong programs, and leaves a university without distinctive advantages over similar institutions.

Strength can be an inherited strong chemistry department. It may be a champion in environmental science. It may be a specially designed simulation classroom. It may be a special endowment (for example, dedicated to the Classics Department) or a large foundation grant, as is the case in our Health Promotion Program.

Once an area of strength is identified, still more money is invested there. Rather than directly strengthening a somewhat weak physical education department, we invested in the program in health promotion and moved from a physical education to a health promotion requirement.

We had in Asheville an eager and financially willing Jewish community, so a Jewish studies center was launched. Our simulation lab has drawn the national headquarters for a related professional association, and we have made space for them on a very overcrowded campus. The academic and entrepreneurial acumen of a single faculty member brought to us the International Mossbauer Effect Data Center.

Pursue the Comparative Advantage. Each college must identify and nourish its "marketable difference." Distinctive programs should be emphasized—programs that can be performed here better than elsewhere because of conditions not frequently replicated in other colleges. For example, UNCA's strategic plan highlights the humanities program because we possess a twenty-three-year tradition of interdisciplinary team teaching, specially designed classrooms, and the disciplinary distribution of faculty to support such an effort. UNCA offers a major in atmospheric science because Asheville is home to the National Weather Archives. UNCA's Center for Creative Retirement builds on its location in a retirement mecca and its traditionally older student body.

Program coherence and cognate strengths can provide comparative advantage. It is easier to build a strong nursing program at institutions with medical schools. Strong public policy institutes are rarely built from weak political science departments.

Ensure Broad Ownership of the Vision. Colleges move in new directions only if most of their multiple constituencies fail to object. No constituency can act alone; many hold the power to stall and veto an action. Similarly, no constituency by itself owns the expertise to frame the best possible action, but most constituencies, through focused advice, can improve the plan.

For bold strategic plans to be both wise and feasible, broad involvement and ownership are essential. Usually, this means extensive consultation among multiple constituencies concerning debatable planned actions, and it means leadership that can accommodate good suggestions and reject inappropriate ones. When Fred Starr first assumed the presidency of Oberlin College (where participatory government is extensive), he arranged for ten-year time series to be prepared for twenty comparison institutions on fifty or so variables, such as standardized test scores of incoming and graduating students. He asked both the trustees and the faculty to point him toward the tables that they most wanted changed, and then he went to work. Starr's approach illustrates an effective way to ensure broad ownership.

Aim High. Students stretch and learn most when they trust the expertise, the currency, and the sincerity of their professors and the resources (such as the library) on which they rely. Donors prefer to back "winning" institutions of demonstrable quality, not dying or mediocre ones. Thus, an institution's ambitions must reflect its resource capacity; it must be selective in what it undertakes, so that it may accomplish its goals well— distinctively well.

At an institution like UNCA, "aiming high" means selecting a few programmatic areas in which national and international acclaim is attainable. It means setting minimum quality standards in all domains and refusing to take any nonreversible action when the threshold quality is not attainable. It means drawing bigger and more ambitious plans from risky but achievable dreams. Often it means working back to the present from a dream of the future, rather than building incrementally from the present to the future.

Maintain Integrity with Basic Educational Convictions. Embedded in the heritage of every college is a fundamental set of educational convictions. Most faculty leadership groups and most presidents come to their positions with sets of educational convictions, and the strategic plan must in all its aspects reflect those convictions. That is integrity.

UNCA's guiding convictions include firm beliefs that a broad and rigorous liberal arts education is appropriate preparation for both life and career, that students must become involved with learning in order to optimize their experience, and that an environment where students trust the quality of their college experience is essential to inspiring maximum learning.

Strategies

Getting specific is the challenge. Which strengths should be pursued? Where are the strongest comparative advantages? Which dreams are most fundable? Aim how high? Broaden ownership how often?

At UNCA, the strategic plan is an untidy collection of reports, each defining an aspect of the aspiration. The script has evolved as ideas have been dropped, added, changed, implemented. When planning began in 1984, the decision about which strategies to pursue right away used as a primary criterion the breadth of involvement needed. Those requiring a more narrow range of expertise, fewer consultations, and a less broad consensus were the first to be implemented. Avoided were domains, such as curriculum, where faculty concerns would appropriately be paramount. Chosen were strategies of augmentation, not pruning, and domains such as physical plant, not tenure policy.

Prompt planning seemed crucial at UNCA. Recent enrollment growth required many new faculty and numerous new buildings. With leadership at last from our neighborhood, our "turn at bat" had come in the legislature.

Strategy 1: Thrust Areas. In my first days as UNCA's new chancellor, I arbitrarily announced that national prominence would be sought in three areas. Each area would receive "off the top of the budget increase funds." This extraordinary, no-questions-asked, discretionary funding was for four years: $50,000 in each of the first two years, and $25,000 in years three and four. As the two-year anniversary approached, one of the three original thrust areas would be "refinanced" for another four-year cycle, and a fourth thrust area would be identified and funded for a four-year cycle.

Beyond discretionary funding, thrust areas would be highlighted in university publications, favored with special attention by officers raising funds, and considered in the strategic planning of all units of the institution. For instance, the criteria for choosing new faculty would include their capacities to support the thrusts.

A key to the swift acceptance of this concept in an environment steeped in extensive faculty involvement in such decisions was that there would be an open competition to select the thrust areas. A faculty committee, the UPC, would make the selections, subject only to administrative ratification. From eleven proposals the UPC chose the interdisciplinary humanities sequence, undergraduate research, and the Health Promotion Program.

For over two decades, all UNCA graduates have been required to

complete a four-course, sixteen-semester-hour general education humanities sequence embracing courses in the ancient world, western civiliza-
tion, the modern world, and the future and the individual. Twenty-six
faculty from eleven departments teach the program. Thrust funds
brought to campus a parade of renowned guest scholars and released a
faculty member to win grant support.

Faculty competition for thrust designation produced a surprise
winner in undergraduate research. Stimulated by the request for proposals, a group of scientists pointed out that UNCA students had been unusu-
ally successful at conferences where undergraduate papers were presented
and that a strong faculty ethic prevailed whereby the most valued research
was that which could involve students. What was happening was that
our young, research-qualified faculty had filled with undergraduates roles
that are usually rationed to graduate students at larger universities,
because graduate students were simply not available.

With the thrust funds for undergraduate research, an administrative
assistant and grant writer was hired, research grants of up to $1,500 were
awarded to students in all disciplinary divisions of the university, and a
journal of undergraduate research was founded. Both an honors program
and a "full-ride" scholarship program (which pays all room, board, and
tuition for four years through outright grants plus the income from
summer internships and a summer research assistantship) were direct
spin-offs. Perhaps the most impressive outcome, however, has been the
organization of the First Annual National Conference on Undergraduate
Research. In the spring of 1987, more than 450 undergraduates came
from 37 states and 130 institutions to read and discuss their research
papers. A new national association has since been formed.

The third winner of thrust designation appointed a professor to test a
new general education course called "Health Promotion." The course
has now been adopted as a graduation requirement for all baccalaureate
students. A $500,000 grant from the Kellogg Foundation and a distinctive
relationship between UNCA and the Mountain Area Health Education
Center greatly aided Health Promotion in the thrust competition.

After two years, the promised reopening of the competition has
occurred. The humanities thrust was chosen for four more years, while
undergraduate research and Health Promotion are moving into their
years of $25,000 funding. Finding no convincing proposal for a fourth
thrust area in this round, the University Planning Council will reopen
competition in 1988–89.

For us, the thrust mechanism has been a relatively inexpensive, flexible mechanism for defining and implementing basic themes within the
strategic plan. It should be adaptable to subunits or to schools within a
university, to universities with larger discretionary funds, and, in a down-
scaled version, to colleges with fewer funds.

Strategy 2: Land Use Master Plan. Properly, a college first states its educational objectives, next identifies needs including physical facilities, and finally funds, locates, and builds the facilities. At UNCA such an order was not to be.

Facility needs were urgent. Funds were available immediately but probably not later. The "window of opportunity" would close if we waited for a constellation of committees and constituencies laboriously to achieve a consensus regarding UNCA's educational plan. Buildings, lots of them, needed to be located before there was a clear picture of UNCA's educational intentions. Within three years, over $30 million of construction and sixty-two additional acres would double the value of the physical plant.

Rather than hurry discussion of "educational futures," UNCA commissioned a land use master plan. We needed $100,000 but got what we could for $40,000. Because land use decisions would precede decisions about educational policies, very broad involvement in the planning was essential.

The land use planning process began with the placement of a giant, twelve-by-sixteen-foot map of the entire campus on the student union lobby's floor. Passersby were encouraged to take off their shoes, crawl over the map, and use magic markers to draw in their ideas for new buildings and roads and sculptures and recreation areas—whatever they wished. Newsprint on easels also provided a means for writing suggestions to the land use planners.

The site planners spent a week on campus and in the Asheville community listening to all who wished to talk, clarifying suggestions from the University Planning Council, surveying topography, and observing use patterns at all hours. After several working conferences with faculty and administrative planning leaders, the architects submitted a preliminary plan, which, in turn, I presented to over forty groups of constituents—students, alumni, faculty, trustees, advisory committees, foundation members, systemwide administrators, former trustees, city council, neighbors, potential investors, service clubs, governmental planning officials, and local architects. These presentations highlighted key planning concepts: growth from 3,000 to 5,000 students within ten years and from 500 to 1,500 dormitory beds; parking to be removed from the interior campus; all academic buildings to be located on current knoll; major reorientation of campus entrance and roads; establishment of gathering places throughout campus; designation of a building zone for "affiliated" organizations; esthetic guidelines for building exteriors; addition of new roads and walkways; preservation of vistas; establishment of "high" and "low" maintenance zones for landscape; and contingency options "if the campus should someday grow to 10,000."

Nothing equals a map of the future campus for catalyzing discussion!

Lively post presentation discussions and memoranda yielded many valuable and several major revisions. Following several well-publicized iterations, the board ratified the final plan, called the General Consensus.

The consideration of physical plans provided a medium for talking with some precision about the consequences of implementing such educational concepts as an intergenerational student body, a spectrum of disciplines, maintenance of a modest size, a liberal arts focus, and increased community service. An unanticipated result was a more ordered and less divisive conversation about guiding educational concepts during the next phase of the planning process. Finding consensus first about physical facilities probably helped provide greater coherence to conceptual planning.

Strategy 3: Guiding Concepts. At the apex of the strategic plan are the "guiding concepts." These unite in a succinct statement key ideas from the mission statement, the UPC minutes, the chancellor's inaugural and state-of-the-university addresses, and the land use master plan. They represent a broad consensus and the widest possible ownership, achieved through a twenty-four-month discussion that began with consideration of a rough draft from the chancellor and the UPC at a year-opening faculty retreat, a special student government meeting, and the annual retreat of the board of trustees. More than twenty groups received formal presentations. Every academic department considered the statement. Final approval involved two endorsements, one of a preliminary version and one of the final version, from the faculty senate as well as adoption by the governing board.

The guiding concepts shape resource allocation. Excerpts follow:

1. UNCA intends to continue to concentrate on undergraduate education.

2. All students, regardless of academic major or career intentions, are and will be universally required to complete a core sequence of study. The academic majors emphasized will largely follow societal and student demand, but the core course methodology will be constant.

3. At UNCA, effort is focused on teaching and service. Research is pursued as a means of strengthening teaching and service.

4. UNCA's strategy is exposure to the new and the unfamiliar in the classroom, library, laboratory, study carrel, and through an array of artistic events, field trips, academic honoraries, special-interest clubs, student government, campus jobs, intramural and athletic contests, and living clusters.

5. UNCA will establish and maintain national prominence in several carefully selected specialty areas.

6. UNCA intends to grow to an ultimate size of 5,000 head count, 3,800 UNCA undergraduates and 1,200 graduate students (enrolled in programs taught by other universities on our campus). An increased proportion should be high-ability students.

7. UNCA efforts will be directed to students from Buncombe and contiguous counties and from throughout the entire state (not only the western third) of North Carolina.

8. Together, the university and central business district, one mile apart, can provide a spectrum of cultural and intellectual resources that reinforce rather than duplicate facilities.

9. UNCA's second role is to serve Asheville and its environs by utilizing its intellectual and physical capacities to enrich the economy and the quality of life for all.

10. UNCA will provide logistic and professional support, including land where appropriate, to kindred organizations, such as the Asheville Graduate Center, the University Botanical Gardens, the United States Forest Service, the Western North Carolina Arboretum, a small business incubator, and the Center for Economic Education.

Strategy 4: Broadening the Ambition and Support for the University. Implementing the strategic plan for a young university, only twenty-five years ago a junior college, requires upscaling ambitions and reaching for a broader range of advocates. Only now are a few beginning to view UNCA as "their" special university. Lacking have been the visibility of larger universities, the loyalty from generations of grateful alumni, and the community pride in flagship institutions. Several approaches have proved fruitful in elevating support.

One important step was the creation of a new Board of Visitors. A group of thirty-five nationally prominent leaders from all sectors of American life serve. The board meets with faculty leadership, especially in the thrust areas, and provides advice, access, and visibility for the advancement of our programs. An investment of $15,000 yearly provides for travel and accommodations for members attending meetings.

There has been a concerted effort to broaden membership on other university boards. The governing board has sought to identify and attract members with a statewide vision and power base. Local advisory committees now relate to each of our management programs and most of our professional curricula. Special advisory groups—examples include the Task Force on Marketing the University, advisory committees for our new Center for Creative Retirement, and the Landscape Master Plan Committee—extend UNCA in still other ways.

For five years, the university has been hosting and managing groups of rising executives, about thirty-five yearly each in Leadership Asheville, Leadership Hendersonville, and Leadership Asheville for Seniors. Employers from both the profit and the nonprofit sectors nominate most participants. Each group spends ten days in the course of a year learning about the public issues facing our community and developing a commitment to do something about them, as well as a network to make action possible. They "graduate" with a commitment to and an understanding not only of the community but also of the university.

The Asheville area is blessed with a very large population of professionals who have migrated to the vicinity in retirement. The newly created Center for Creative Retirement is, among other things, intended to capture some of these talents for our undergraduates and to nurture support from an important new constituency.

New series of humanities guest lecturers and of visiting chief executive officers allow us extensive interaction with frontier thinkers and practitioners and, at the same time, allow our visitors to become advocates for our programs. A massive influx of new ideas has come, as well, from our hosting of the First Annual Conference on Undergraduate Research.

Finally, visits to other campuses broaden UNCA's perspective, its fund of available information, its aspirations, and its external support. Each year several administrative and faculty leaders journey to a "comparable" campus to learn from successes and failures elsewhere.

Strategy 5: Resource Flow Plan. During the 1987–88 academic year, faculty and administrative leaders have been detailing the phasing in of new buildings, the introduction of new programs, and the generation and allocation of new resources. Already the time is nearing when a new study, to prepare for an accreditation visit, will supplement the strategic plan.

Conclusion

When on the move, a university wisely conducts several studies of where it is headed. Each study should take advantage of "outside" as well as "inside" perspectives. Conscious efforts must be made to raise and broaden the institution's aspirations. Instinct and tradition are poor guides when a rapid transition is in progress. Reasoned planning is needed. A strategic plan loosely confederates multiple studies and reports, each building on its predecessor. The order may not be as important as the intention.

The risks, of emotion and career, are high, but so are the rewards and satisfactions of strategic planning. With such planning, a university can in fact undergo rapid enhancement while enriching the education of present students.

David G. Brown is chancellor of the University of North Carolina at Asheville.

Articulation and communication of a strategic self-understanding has provided Centre College with the basis for making decisions.

Centre College of Kentucky

Richard L. Morrill

Centre College entered the 1980s with an established position of leadership among small liberal arts colleges in the mid South. Distinguished and loyal alumni, a collegial and committed faculty, bright and energetic students, and excellent facilities were all part of the college's profile well known in Kentucky and selectively in other parts of the country. A highly successful three-year Fund for the Future campaign initiated in 1979 by a farsighted president and board of trustees had attracted $12 million in cash contributions and $22 million in documented wills and other deferred gifts, effectively guaranteeing the institution's future.

Although Centre's dominant position was a stable one, the college faced problems pressing many strong institutions like it. Applications for admission were in some decline, enrollment had fallen over five years from above 800 to just below 700, entering student test scores and class ranks had eroded, an accumulated current fund deficit of over $300,000 was beginning to pinch, the percentage of students on financial aid was rising rapidly, and the recent shift of much of the endowment to high-yield, fixed-income investments in order to increase current income was potentially sacrificing profits from the appreciation of equities. As elsewhere, salaries had suffered from inflation and were comparatively low even by regional standards. The capital campaign had, however, produced a sense of momentum, and there was the imminent prospect of greatly increased endowment funding through the sale and reinvestment of high-appreciated, low-yield securities.

D. W. Steeples (ed.). *Successful Strategic Planning: Case Studies.*
New Directions for Higher Education, no. 64. San Francisco: Jossey-Bass, Winter 1988.

When I arrived as the college's new president in early summer 1982, the moment seemed especially promising to initiate strategic planning. My earlier experience at several different institutions involved various approaches to long-range planning, and I had experimented with strategic planning in a prior presidency. In that first long and quiet summer, I spent many hours with our vice-president and general secretary spelling out the goals and the procedures we might develop in a full-blown strategic planning process. Since there was no formal office of institutional research and no professional staff in the president's office, I turned to the general secretary and his staff for the administrative leadership of the project. We were soon able to define the magnitude of the task, particularly in terms of the time-consuming work in data gathering and analysis that eventually would be required. We decided to collect information on various aspects of institutional operations from Centre, from a group of nationally prominent liberal arts colleges, and from a set of strong institutions in our region. Perhaps most significant in the research process was the creation of a whole series of ratios and proportions that allowed us to make direct comparisons between institutions. Other procedural steps developed concurrently with the research work.

Issues of Process and Procedure

We decided that strategic planning, to succeed, needed to involve a significant cross section of the campus community, including members of the faculty, administrative staff, and student body. At Centre, as on most campuses, the way a decision is made is as important as the decision itself. We created a Planning and Priorities Committee of thirteen members, with the president serving ex officio. Five senior administrators reporting to the president, two faculty members from each of the college's three academic divisions, and two students comprised the committee. This group was asked to play a major role in developing a written strategic planning document.

Simultaneously, an active relationship was initiated with the chair of the board of trustees' Committee on Long-Range Planning. This individual possessed a strong background in corporate planning and was both knowledgeable and enthusiastic about the possibilities of strategic planning at Centre. Soon enough the board body became, simply, the Planning Committee. Regular contact followed with the committee's chair, and, as research proceeded, information was provided to the committee. It began to meet regularly prior to each meeting of the governing board.

The First Year: Research. During the first year, the main task was to consider studies of such matters as admissions, finances, salaries, retention, fund raising, library, and so forth. While the Planning and Priorities Committee was settling on how best to present the comparative data, it was also gaining a sharper awareness of the specific environmental challenges and opportunities facing the college. As the first academic year drew to a close, the committee was ready to write a substantive analysis of Centre's comparative position in the environment.

The Second Year: Writing the Narrative. The beginning of the second year was the busiest and most telling time in the planning process. Over the summer the committee chair, Centre's vice-president and general secretary, drafted large sections of a strategic planning document. The work drew on research data, committee discussions, conversations with the president, and consultation with the chair of the board's Planning Committee.

Next, I revised and expanded the document before sending it to the campus Planning and Priorities Committee. After the committee forwarded written reactions, the text underwent significant, but not substantive, changes. When a second draft was ready, the committee discussed and modified it in two or three lengthy meetings as well as an all-day retreat. At the retreat, a consultant from a university in a neighboring state led a discussion of institutional culture and took the group through exercises that both paralleled and supported the draft document's conclusions about mission and purposes. This visit resulted from Centre's participation in a national study of values and decision making in higher education sponsored by the Society for Values in Higher Education.

Following the committee's approval, the document, now some 200 pages in length, received consideration from Centre's academic governing body, the College Council, consisting of all faculty members and student and staff representatives. This was done in two meetings, which resulted in the approval in principle of the strategic plan.

Finally, toward the end of year two, the document went to the board's Planning Committee and to the full board. Both the committee and the board readily endorsed the draft, the board by a unanimous vote.

Collegial Process. The processes used in preparing and approving the plan are not unusual for a collegial institution like Centre. The document resulted from joint faculty and administration efforts, although, given the nature of the enterprise, administrators led. As a new president, I was comfortably able to be very involved myself, which might not be typical at either a larger institution or in a less open and trusting environment.

Academic strategic planning proves to be a long and somewhat cumbersome task. One must build in from the start the opportunity for various constituencies to influence the outcome and to express their concerns. When openness and initiative, discussion and action are in proper balance, a whole series of shared assumptions is formed across the institution that can help create a unified and focused community.

Institutional Self-Discovery

Page nine of the study that came to be titled *Centre College: Empowerment Through Liberal Education* offers this definition of strategic planning: "For Centre College strategic planning is a process of institutional self-discovery and articulation in relation to the constraints of available resources and environmental pressures and opportunities." The statement contains the two distinctive emphases characteristic of strategic planning. At Centre, though, the major focus has been the process of self-discovery. Analysts of organizational life who emphasize the decisive importance of an institution's values and culture have much to contribute to an effective program of strategic planning. A genuinely strategic approach to Centre's self-definition proved to be extremely worthwhile, even though the institution already knew itself well in many respects. Seeing Centre compared to other institutions and in the context of a changing environment lent a new significance to detailed descriptions of institutional role and purpose. They were discovered to represent distinctive choices that set this college apart from all others. Self-knowledge is the beginning of wisdom for institutions as well as for individuals, especially during periods of rapid change.

The task of discovering an institution's identity is both simple and complex. It involves a work of true intellectual synthesis using many types of information and methods of analysis. Adequate quantitative data are essential, especially for comparisons among colleges. It quickly becomes clear that no one set of facts about an institution, or even one aspect of an institution, tells anything like the whole story. There remain enormous variations in the ways in which institutions collect and report information, striking regional differences in the cost of living, plausible explanations for apparently extreme results, and so on. Good comparative data are useful in raising questions, in stimulating thought, and in defining a framework for further study. Frequently, various facts and figures begin to reveal a set of institutional values and commitments that characterize an institution's sense of itself, its special story or saga. Effective strategic planning also involves a great deal of listening, of hearing stories of fulfillment and disappointment, of discerning the norms by which people assess one another's conduct even without knowing that they do so, of eliciting and explicating assumptions and images. On most campuses there are key images, metaphors, and values that define an institution's history and aspirations. Although these are often vague and may lack full consensus, they offer essential clues toward defining an institution's purpose.

Pride. It was very common to hear both on and off campus that Centre probably was "the best academic institution" in the state among those offering undergraduate liberal arts programs. How to prove such a statement may be debated endlessly, but in the strategic planning process that image was found to be vital in explaining much about the college. Centre is a place of pride. Students express pride about how hard they work in comparison with their friends who attend other institutions. Alumni take satisfaction in leading the country in participation in annual giving. Pride figures in the unusual degree of collegiality among the faculty and between the faculty and the administration. There is an unstated sense that the work that is being done truly matters, at least in part because it sets a standard for achievement in our part of the country. Pride proves to be not an empty boast but something that defines and explains much of the college's culture.

Smallness. Centre is small, even very small. The quantitative data showed that this small size created some relative inefficiencies as well as some important opportunities. Most of the implications of smallness, though, were discovered beyond the data, through conversations both in and outside the committee. Smallness at a college like Centre is really a symbol of the intensity of student access to the resources of the institution. With few barriers or limits, the time and attention of the faculty are focused directly and primarily on the student. There are countless intensive transactions in the way teachers grade papers with long comments, hold endless personal conferences to review work, and offer daily personal encouragement. A well-stocked and well-built campus is shared by only 800 students with a rich per-person level of access to facilities and equipment. People often express their reasons for loyalty to the college in terms of the intensely personal access they have enjoyed to key persons and resources; this is the meaning that "smallness" takes on in Centre's story.

Size and Goals. The strategic analysis of size also demonstrated that colleges under 1,000 or any other arbitrary number are not by definition financially or academically at risk. Size alone is not an adequate measure of the use and availability of resources or of the nature of a college's purposes and commitments. An institution's size should follow from the goals it sets for itself. A college like Centre has only one purpose and one program—undergraduate study in the arts and sciences. There are no professional or vocational offerings, no graduate programs, no continuing education courses, and no research institutes. The crucial consideration is not large or small size, but appropriate size relative to the goals and ambitions of institutional life.

Strategic Implications. An integrative analysis of facts and values reveals the strategic implications of an institution's self-understanding. Even ritualistic phrases like "liberal arts college" assume new meaning through this kind of inquiry. For example, Centre's commitment to the liberal arts is exclusive, unlike the great majority of institutions that use the same term to describe programs that often are strongly career-oriented or heavily and narrowly preprofessional. Centre also presupposes that liberal education by definition must involve both a breadth and a depth of study and, further, that it should seek to engage students in the encompassing task of human development. Although there are no pat formulas through which these broader aims of education can be achieved, Centre continues to intend that education be understood as a form of human empowerment. Clarifying what a college intends by the liberal arts offers definite benefits when it comes time to plan and assess academic programs.

These and many other fundamental terms received an analysis that pushed for distinctiveness and concreteness. Although planners used the normal lexicon of institutional self-description, they sought to move away from empty phrases toward determinate meanings. Words like "quality" and "excellence" underwent the same kind of scrutiny and were translated into specifiable characteristics and results.

This systematic approach to institutional self-understanding produced two important consequences: First, people commonly reported that they were hearing and seeing very familiar things as if for the first time. A sense of confidence and shared commitment emerged quite strongly, as people concluded that a reasonably accurate statement had been made of the institution as they had experienced it but had perhaps not been able to articulate fully. Second, when the time for making choices among attractive options arrived, an effective self-definition provided a useful framework for doing so.

The Aspirations to Become a National Model

Centre's strategic planning study contained five chapters: "The Era of Competition"; "Education as Empowerment: Mission"; "Facets of Institutional Distinctiveness"; "Centre as a National Model of Excellence"; and "Financial Resources." Chapter Three, a comprehensive analysis of the strengths and weaknesses of most of the college's major programs and operational divisions, was by far the longest. It systematically reviewed everything from financial position to the curriculum, drawing on recent studies, reports, and discussions within the committee. Comparative data from other institutions and the results of the work on institutional identity helped to focus this discussion. Usually, the discussion of a given educational or administrative program concluded with the development of as precise a statement of goals as possible.

A pivotal question in Centre's strategic planning concerned the level of institutional aspiration. To seek or promise objectives that were too demanding would make the whole effort an exercise in empty rhetoric, a characteristic not uncommon in institutional self-studies. Yet to fail to crystallize the many signs of institutional energy and momentum would be to miss an opportunity that might not soon recur. An environmental analysis had persuaded everyone that, in this era of intense competitiveness for higher education, efforts directed toward simply maintaining the status quo would undoubtedly result in relative decline. Strong institutions were becoming ever stronger and showing remarkable resilience in competing for a declining number of students and a fixed amount of resources. One of the most significant decisions, then, was to try to voice Centre's level of aspiration in a way that was both realistic and inspiring. Above all, the description of institutional aspiration had to be useful in guiding other strategic choices.

The concept that was chosen to sum up Centre's aspirations sounds all too familiar, but it has actually functioned in a distinctive way. Centre aims fundamentally to become a model of national consequence for institutions of its size and type. It chose this primary goal for many reasons. One was to "take on" the fairly widespread skepticism about the possibility of colleges under 1,000 being viable and of the highest academic quality. Another was that a wide variety of criteria can be used to establish Centre as a national model; this aspiration does not mean that Centre must draw students proportionately from all across the country. Neither does it connote instant universal recognition, which is virtually impossible for any small institution. Rather, becoming a national model means that Centre should offer possibilities worthy of emulation throughout the nation by colleges of a similar size and type.

Measurable Goals

Ultimately, Centre defined the notion of becoming a national model not by rhetoric but by a series of nearly fifty measures that would collectively portray what it would mean to be an institution of national consequence. In a way that now seems much more risky than it did at the time, the strategic plan developed measurable goals for all of the major areas of the college, such as curriculum, student admission into graduate and professional schools, the Norton Center for the Arts (the college's unusual and ambitious performing and student arts center), salaries and resources for faculty, student life, admissions and enrollment both in size and quality, academic resources such as library and computers, support staff programs, financial position, campus facilities, and so forth. However debatable this list of measures, certainly an institution that possesses these fifty-odd characteristics is a very strong institution indeed and a model for others.

The creation of a list of carefully considered measurable goals holds important consequences for decision making and strategic planning. One result is the generation of enormous pressure on a college's leadership; at the same time, verifiable progress toward attainment of the goals stirs a sense of confidence and credibility throughout the institution. People become believers in themselves, in the college, and in the integrity of the strategic planning process. As crucial everyday and periodic decisions refer again and again to strategic planning goals, a sense of coherence and purpose becomes part of decision making. For example, a goal to improve faculty salaries to the seventy-fifth percentile for similar institutions is a stern budgetary taskmaster; decisions about tuition levels and the use of resources must be related to that goal, since much of the budget is tied to faculty personnel costs. Success, however, replaces traditional patterns of academic skepticism with enthusiasm and trust, even though many campus citizens predictably continue to view good results as only what is deserved and to be expected.

Operating by the Plan

Centre's strategic plan has been neither a document on a shelf nor a bible that people consult daily when arriving at work. The product, not just the process, has been important. The plan's major goals and principles have worked themselves into every aspect of decision making on campus. This has been especially true of the major decisions relating to the annual budget and to the development and implementation of annual plans within each area of college operations. Each senior officer prepares an annual report that is intended to be a strategic plan in miniature, although that goal is not always achieved. These annual reports lay the foundation for lengthy meetings with the president in which objectives are established, progress is reviewed, and problems are discussed. Where needed, special committees and task forces have been formed to address the problems and opportunities revealed in this planning activity.

The strategic plan has proved to be invaluable in any number of other operational areas. For example, the college has enjoyed notable success in securing major grants from national foundations, including $3.5 million from the F. W. Olin Foundation; in some cases, grant proposals were able to draw directly from the contents of the strategic plan. In addition, each year the board of trustees has formally reviewed progress toward reaching each of the goals that the strategic plan has set.

One of the most significant consequences of the strategic plan was the decision to initiate the Campaign for Centre only four years after successfully completing the Fund for the Future. The plan was largely responsible for engendering a sense of enthusiasm and commitment among the trustees, who would be expected to contribute substantially to the new capital effort. The critical questions of the campaign's need and purposes, which are the most crucial elements in any successful development effort, had already been addressed in the planning study. Although a few alumni at first had some trouble understanding exactly what is meant by "becoming a national model," the college's success in reaching its goals has validated the plan's high aspirations.

Assessing the Plan

As I have stressed, one important aspect of Centre's approach to strategic planning has been the use of measurable results. Examples of the progress in reaching key goals in the four years since goal definition and three since final board approval include the following:

- Applications have risen from 500 to 1,000 yearly, exceeding the goal of 800.
- The 290 entering students in fall 1987 surpassed the target of 225 freshmen and 20 transfers.
- Centre has achieved the objective of an entering class of 60 percent in the top 10 percent of the high school class, with average American College Testing (ACT) scores in the ninetieth percentile.
- The student body has made only modest progress toward greater geographic and ethnic diversity (only 2 or 3 percent are minority students; 69 percent are in-state students).
- Enrollment has risen beyond the projected 775–800, to 850–860.
- Active Centre recruiting, fund-raising, and career-planning networks have been created in Atlanta, Nashville, Cincinnati, Knoxville, and Washington, D.C.
- The annual fund has grown by much more than the projected 10 percent yearly, and alumni participation in the fund, at 75.3 percent, leads the nation.
- Centre has won increased national media attention, with significant articles in major periodicals and a listing in every major selective admissions guide.
- The library will undergo a $1.2 million renovation and gain increased funds for acquisitions.
- During the five years ending with 1988, Centre will have established two campus networks of personal computers and purchased other scientific and computing equipment that satisfies foreseeable needs.
- Faculty salaries have risen 50 percent in five years, from the fortieth-to-sixtieth percentile range for each rank in the American Association of University Professors survey and from 5 percent below to 7 percent above national averages for baccalaureate institutions.
- The $335,000 current fund deficit has been eliminated, and a $1 million plant and operating reserve has been established.

- The goals and rationale of general education were reviewed in 1987; one result will be a one-course reduction in teaching loads in 1988–89.

In all, results have exceeded the original projections in about 40 percent of the cases, have met goals in another 40 percent, and have fallen short in the remaining 20 percent. As happens in any use of strategic planning, unanticipated events have altered goals and even some of the premises. At Centre, reality set aside our projection that the optimum size for the college would be in the 775 to 800 zone and required us to move the goal upward to the area of 825 to 850. Our projection of the yield of accepted students in the spring of 1987 was incorrect by about four percentage points, creating a much larger freshman class than was anticipated. A new dormitory for fifty students is currently being planned, a prospect that would have seemed ludicrous when the strategic plan was first drafted. Further, significant space limitations that existed in classrooms and laboratories and in the library have become worse than was foreseen when the plan was adopted. They are in the process of being removed through use of the $3.5 million grant from the F. W. Olin Foundation.

Results at Centre and elsewhere have also revealed that the outlook for higher education, and especially for strong and selective colleges, is much more positive than was expected. Strong national and regional emphases on improvement in the quality of education, a need for competitiveness in the world marketplace, the extraordinary loyalty of alumni and friends, renewed interest in liberal education, and other factors have created a positive niche within an environment that continues to be negative and threatening in many fundamental ways.

After three to four years, the details and specifics of the strategic plan are clearly out of date. It is time to reanalyze the college's situation and its specific objectives for the future. Next year will see the development of a new series of goals that will then enter into the fabric of institutional decision making. Some of the earlier conceptual work analyzing the environment and the college's sense of itself will have to be examined again, but it is doubtful that fundamental changes will occur. In formulating the next plan, Centre will especially need to strike a careful balance between goals and available resources, because it is not likely that a capital campaign can be developed so soon after two intensive efforts in one decade. Needs for new programs will have to be measured against the availability of carefully targeted sources of funding. Happily, it is improbable that there will be any needs for construction in the foreseeable future, and several renovations, although desirable, are not yet mandatory. Moreover, some of the most expensive requirements of the plan, such as salary improvement, are close to being satisfied. It is, then, with some sense of anticipation and enthusiasm that we approach the preparation of a second planning document. We are convinced that strategic planning has made the single most significant administrative contribution to Centre College's present level of strength and achievement.

Richard L. Morrill is president of Centre College.

The University of Louisville's successful strategic planning effort, in which presidential leadership played a central role, shows how strategic planning can be a powerful process for making key decisions about a university's future.

The University of Louisville

Donald C. Swain

Strategic planning began at the University of Louisville (U of L) in 1983. I was personally involved in virtually every step of the planning process. After pondering what I could write that might be useful to senior university administrators, I decided on a memoir of my own involvement, focusing on what I learned about strategic planning as a result of my experiences at the U of L.

Still a relatively new university president in 1983, I had a mandate from the board of trustees to provide strong executive leadership. My previous administrative positions, in the University of California system, had given me extensive experience in long-range academic planning, but I had never attempted strategic planning.

Planning had a bad reputation at the university in 1983. It was perceived as a circular, abstract, endless process that had little or no relevance to decision making. Yet the U of L, which was still making the attitudinal transition from an independent, municipally supported university to a state-supported institution, faced in the 1980s difficult problems that demanded carefully planned solutions.

The University of Louisville had a long and distinguished history, but it had not come to terms with its "urban mission" as defined by Kentucky's coordinating board, the Council on Higher Education, in 1977. It was a large university, with about 20,000 students, but it was not behaving like a major institution of higher learning, with confidence

D. W. Steeples (ed.). *Successful Strategic Planning: Case Studies.*
New Directions for Higher Education, no. 64. San Francisco: Jossey-Bass, Winter 1988.

and high expectations. It offered a wide range of undergraduate and master's programs, doctorates in seventeen selected disciplines, and professional degrees in medicine, law, dentistry, and engineering. But it lacked focus and momentum. It needed to emphasize its role as one of the state's two research universities. It urgently needed to broaden its support in the Louisville metropolitan area and the state. It clearly needed to develop a strategy for coping with change and for filling a distinctive niche in the Kentucky system of higher education.

Likewise, it was clear that I, as a new president, needed to lay out a road map—a strategic plan—delineating my main leadership goals. The university's imperatives converged with my own as chief executive officer. The time was right for launching an ambitious strategic planning process.

Establishing a Planning Protocol

Like many other universities, the University of Louisville is devoted to procedure. Our first task was to establish the procedure by which to carry out strategic planning.

Executive Leadership. I started talking with the board of trustees about strategic goals in 1982-83. Several trustees were successful chief executive officers who had employed strategic planning in their own organizations. They urged me to be among the first university presidents to explore strategic planning. Out of these discussions came a document entitled "Goal and Objectives of the President and the Board of Trustees of the University of Louisville." It stated that the university's goal should be to become "one of the best urban universities in the country by comparison to other leading urban universities." It also identified some of the essential, specific objectives to be accomplished if the U of L were to achieve this goal.

When asked to comment on the document, the faculty senate reacted not by disagreeing with the goal but rather by expressing skepticism about the wisdom of allowing the board and the president to take the lead in such matters. Nevertheless, the trustees proudly adopted the statement on September 26, 1983. Looking back, I can see that this was a crucial step. Board members and the CEO had committed themselves to a simple, specific goal and to the kind of planning necessary to achieve it.

The staff of the Office of Planning and Budget and I had implemented a quick and controversial process in 1981-82 to plan for a required 6 percent budget cut. I had a sense that strong executive leadership was essential to overcome the robust centrifugal forces within any university. I had read George Keller's (1983) *Academic Strategy* and had discovered that certain other institutions of higher learning were moving in similar directions—that is, applying the concept of strategic planning to a complex university setting, confronting tough problems openly, and depending on forceful executive leadership to ensure the urgency and high priority of the project.

Faculty Advisory Role. To achieve a greater administrative and faculty understanding of strategic planning, the director of planning and budget brought a well-qualified National Center for Higher Education Management Systems consultant, Dr. Robert Shirley, to the campus for two seminars on strategic planning at which initial proposals about procedure were discussed. Those seminars, led by an objective expert, helped educate the prospective participants and gave them a chance to voice their concerns and make suggestions.

We revised our proposed procedures as a result of these discussions. The main concerns of the faculty senate were that the faculty representatives on all major planning committees should be elected by the faculty as a whole and that the faculty should be deeply involved in all phases of the planning process, including the decision making.

I argued that if strategic planning were to be effective, the faculty committee participants had to be our most imaginative, most perceptive faculty, those whose personalities and frame of reference would enable them to rise to a universitywide view and avoid narrower, turf-oriented perspectives. I stated my conviction that elected faculty representatives would not necessarily reflect these characteristics and reiterated my intention to appoint the committees from slates of nominees submitted by the faculty senate, the deans, vice-presidents, and others. The faculty senate, after protracted discussion, acquiesced reluctantly to this approach.

While agreeing that faculty involvement in strategic planning was critical, I pointed out that *The Redbook* (the university's governance document) conferred decision-making authority on the president, not the faculty. My suggestion was that we should divide the universitywide planning process into two phases: a preliminary and advisory phase in which faculty would be centrally involved and a decision-making phase. In the latter, the university's "regularly established procedures" would be used. I would not appoint any "supercommittees" to make decisions; the president would make them after seeking, as *The Redbook* required, the comments and advice of the faculty senate, the staff senate, and the student senate. In the end, the faculty senate accepted this approach, although a brisk debate ensued and some members expressed fear that the president would dominate the planning process.

I believe that these procedural decisions—to reject elected committees representing various vested interests and to retain the president's role as decision maker at the end of a prescribed consultative process—were crucial to our later success.

Preliminary and Advisory Phase

Early in the fall term of 1983, the active planning process began. After wide consultation, I issued some guidelines, dubbed "The Givens," that listed a set of constraints that were beyond the power of the university to change. Among these were the applicable state statutes and regulations, the mission assigned to the University of Louisville by the Council on Higher Education, the state's biennial appropriations act, and the president's and board's "Goal and Objectives" statement.

Next, I appointed three important planning committees. The first was the Environmental Analysis Work Group, chaired by a faculty member from the School of Business, Dr. C. Aaron Kelley, an expert in strategic planning. (He also served as a consultant in the later stages of the process.) This body consisted of faculty chosen especially for their broad perspective and competence in certain specific specialties (for example, marketing, economic forecasting, and metropolitan and state government), and some of the best business executives in Louisville who had experience in strategic planning. Their report was excellent, pointing to both special opportunities and dangerous pitfalls. It earned the respect of the people who later utilized its findings in the planning process.

The second committee that I appointed was charged to survey and analyze the university community's attitudes and values. This was a clear-cut assignment, calling for individuals with recognized expertise in survey techniques and statistical methods. Composed of well-respected, unquestionably competent faculty members, this group used a standard instrument, the Institutional Goals Inventory, to survey faculty, students, staff, administrators, and board members. The results were accepted without conflict.

The third committee was the Academic Advisory Group, chaired by the acting university provost and made up of seven faculty, one student, and one staff member. Its task was to study the "Givens," the external environment analysis, the institutional values report and the suggestions from the three senates and to make recommendations to the president about the strategic directions that the university should take for the next ten years. The committee held open forums to discuss its draft report. After receiving vigorous comments and many suggestions for change, it produced a final report that revealed a responsiveness to those who commented seriously on the first draft.

I had instructed the unit heads to submit analyses of the strengths and weaknesses of their units. To promote candor, the planning and budget staff and I decided not to distribute these reports very widely. I made them available to the Academic Advisory Group, but they turned out to be uneven and, frankly, not as useful as I had hoped.

The Academic Advisory Group lagged behind its schedule and asked for an extension of its due date, which I approved. I found it generally wise to forgive a little slippage in the schedule, as long as the committee continued to struggle genuinely with its assignment.

The Academic Advisory Group submitted its report in June 1984. The document dealt with many of the issues facing the university, and it contained the grist for a universitywide strategic plan. It proposed changes, such as linking more closely to the Louisville urban area, expanding basic and applied research, establishing cooperative relationships with business, government, and other external agencies, and reorganizing certain academic units.

The report, though substantial, was not crisply focused, nor was it tough-minded enough, at least in its final form. It was, however, a legitimate effort to look to the future and propose a strategy. Unlike a traditional long-range planning report, it offered recommendations based on the environment in which the university operated and the constraints that, in fact, existed. It assumed that plans, once adopted, would be implemented. This was a breakthrough at the University of Louisville.

I assigned the Office of Planning and Budget to provide staff assistance to these three committees. This assured continuity and fundamental planning competency in these indispensable early advisory efforts. The fact that the Office of Planning and Budget already had a reputation for effectiveness and a service orientation was an undeniable asset.

The preliminary and advisory phase concluded in the summer of 1984. At that point, the focus shifted from collecting ideas and seeking advice to the hard work of making decisions and constructing a universitywide strategy. My personal involvement had been decisive, I believe, in establishing the initial framework for planning and in bolstering the start-up stage. It would become a central feature of the decision-making phase.

One of my earliest actions as president was to instruct the director of planning and budget to report directly to me, signaling my intent not to delegate the planning and budget functions to anyone else. Planning and budget, I thought, were the president's main tools of internal university leadership. This concept would now be tested.

The Decision-Making Phase

There was intensive strategic planning activity in my office during the summer of 1984. Working with the staff of the Office of Planning and Budget, I extracted the most promising ideas generated in the preliminary and advisory phase and developed an ambitious calendar for completing the overall strategic plan. I designated the President's Administrative Cabinet (PAC), made up essentially of the provost, vice-presidents, and deans, as the main staff group that would advise me on planning. This was a well-recognized, existing group—not a super-committee—which was consistent with my agreement to use the "regular process" of consultation in this phase.

I quickly learned that the PAC was ungainly for offering planning advice. It was too large and made up of strong advocates from each unit. It had difficulty dealing with universitywide issues, especially those that offered advantages to some units and disadvantages to others.

More and more I used the "president's staff," a smaller group composed of the provost, vice-presidents, director of planning and budget, university counsel, and my personal assistant, as my sounding board. I worked closely with this group to develop proposed preliminary themes for the strategic plan, which I then presented to the PAC for reaction and discussion. This approach facilitated matters and allowed the PAC to act as a critical evaluator, whose task it was to ferret out mistaken assumptions or conclusions once an idea was ready for discussion. The PAC, acting as a whole, did not generate many new ideas.

The president's staff and I, assisted by the planning and budget staff, spent an intensive two weeks in September 1984 drafting a document entitled "Universitywide Strategic Directions," which I presented to the PAC for review. The draft carefully and deliberately drew themes from the report of the Academic Advisory Group. It added new ideas that emerged from the dynamics of my discussions with the president's staff and the PAC. By mid October, it was ready for distribution to the faculty, staff, and students for review and comment.

Open Discussions. Openness is generally a virtue in strategic planning. I convened and presided personally at an open forum on strategic planning on October 16, 1984, to begin a two-month period of debate about the draft strategic directions document. I summarized the draft, answered questions, and invited participation. Afterward, I sent copies to the faculty, staff, and student senates for comments and suggestions. I put copies on reserve in the library for others who were genuinely interested and wanted to submit responses. I asked each dean to discuss the draft with his or her faculty and to submit the unit's comments and recommendations. Even more important, I asked the units to identify their top priorities in the draft. Likewise, I requested that the provost and vice-presidents discuss the draft with their staff subordinates and send me their comments and priorities.

In December 1984, I held two open forums to solicit reactions to the draft from individuals within the university community. In the great tradition of a university, there were open disagreements, but the forums took place in an atmosphere of general good humor and tolerance, partly evoked by the blizzard that hit Louisville on the day of the first forum. By the end of December 1984, I had received hundreds of comments and suggested changes.

Responsive Revision. In January 1985, I took the lead in revising the draft, with the help of the president's staff and the Office of Planning and Budget. I adopted as many suggested changes as possible without allowing the document to lose its focus and decisiveness. The planning and budget staff informed every group that sent in suggestions which ideas were accepted and why the others could not be accepted.

I distributed a revised draft of "Universitywide Strategic Directions" for another review in February. I wanted the faculty, students, and staff to know about the changes that were proposed and to have one final opportunity to catch any significant, previously undetected flaws. After a final, fairly simple revision, I prepared the document for submission to the board of trustees in April 1985.

The Plan. "Universitywide Strategic Directions" stated its assumptions, proposed a series of five-year goals, and identified specific objectives to be achieved over the next two years. In brief, it laid out a strategy that would improve overall quality; increase the emphasis on research; enhance the quality of instruction; stress the urban mission; make the campuses more welcoming, friendly, and service-oriented; adapt to change quickly and responsibly; improve the effectiveness of management; and attain increased institutional standing.

In final form, the printed document filled only sixteen pages. Brief, straightforward documents are advantageous in strategic planning. More people read and understand them if they are short and pointed.

I had periodically briefed the trustees during the fall term of 1984 about the draft document and the issues under discussion. From the beginning, they were staunch supporters of strategic planning. All of this strengthened my leadership and conveyed to interested faculty and other groups that the board and the president were moving together toward a goal that they perceived as fundamentally important.

The trustees unanimously and enthusiastically approved "Universitywide Strategic Directions" in principle. The university now had officially adopted an umbrella strategy.

Strategic Planning at the Unit Level

I had taken it for granted that strategic planning would be more effective if a general institutionwide strategy could be established first; later, the units could develop their own more detailed plans. This planning sequence in fact provided guidance to the units and encouraged them to contribute their own ideas and energy. The only strictly enforced requirement was that the unit plans must help move the institution toward its overall strategic goals.

I had originally expected the vice-presidents to prepare "implementation plans" for key universitywide operational areas—enrollment, finance, facilities, admissions and student recruitment, human resources, and operations. These proved to be unnecessary, as the "Universitywide Strategic Directions" document, in the end, encompassed implementation. To the applause of the vice-presidents, I announced that they would not need to produce the implementation plans.

At first, I was not personally involved in working with the academic units to develop their strategies. However, the process of preparing the academic unit plans, which began in the summer of 1985, got bogged down in the fall. The unit plans were becoming too detailed and were turning into specific budget requests; the units were not focusing on strategic planning considerations. This distressed me because I had been insisting for two years that strategic planning, not budget decisions, must lead the way.

At about this time, George Keller visited the university to present a seminar on strategic planning. He talked to many of the deans and vice-presidents. I asked him to tell me candidly how the unit planning process was progressing. He confirmed my impression that it was floundering and urged me to take charge personally again. I followed his advice.

I announced to the unit heads that I wanted to bring this phase of strategic planning to a prompt conclusion. I suggested that the draft plan for each unit be considered a working document that could provide ideas and future guidance to the units but that would not be officially approved. What I, as CEO, would approve after meeting with each unit head would be a brief statement of the unit's priorities for action (in no more than three or four pages), summarizing the agreed-on priorities for the next two years. As a follow-up to the meetings, I wrote each unit head stating my expectations about the items that would receive new funds in the next biennium. I instructed them to move ahead expeditiously on the many priority items that required no new funding. I used this approach with both academic and nonacademic units. The deans and vice-presidents concurred that it put the planning process back on track.

We now had the format for our completed strategic plan. "Universitywide Strategic Directions" would constitute Part One. "Priorities for Action" documents from each of the units, as well as a universitywide "Priorities for Action" statement summarizing the priorities that grew out of the preparation of "Universitywide Strategic Directions," would comprise Part Two.

My colleagues and I had learned about the virtues of flexibility in strategic planning. We felt free to modify the procedure itself or even the type of reports required, depending on the unfolding situation. We decided to relax and let strategic planning be a truly dynamic process, as it was intended to be.

I presented the finished plan to the trustees for approval on January 27, 1986. With undisguised pleasure, I summarized the process we had gone through and highlighted selected priorities from the units' statements. The board approved the entire plan in principle and, recognizing the creative ideas and energy embodied in it, asked me to compliment all who had contributed to our successful strategic planning enterprise.

The Aftermath

We took a break from strategic planning for a few months, but, if we seriously intended for plans to drive important budget decisions, we had to update them in time for the next biennial budget request, which would be due in about eighteen months. I announced a schedule for updating the plan. A few muffled groans could be heard from the ranks of the deans.

In the meantime, I found that, yes, having a strategic plan makes a difference in shaping the operating budget. Priorities for funding were already established and agreed to. I held a heavy responsibility to make certain that the link between plans and budgets remained direct and obvious. Unless the CEO insists on this, it will not occur in a large university; there are too many possibilities for trade-offs that move in unplanned directions. Again I found it fortunate that I had not delegated the planning and budget functions.

Conclusions

There are no panaceas in managing a major university, but strategic planning has obviously been a useful tool in moving the University of Louisville systematically toward its goal. I am not suggesting that the style of leadership or the planning approach that worked at the U of L would be successful anywhere else. If the circumstances were similar, perhaps they could be applicable, at least in a minimal sense. A skillful CEO would want to adapt and modify any suggested approach to fit the special circumstances and needs of his or her own institution.

What I learned about strategic planning is clear and categorical:

1. Strong, personal leadership by the CEO is indispensable. Others in the university must recognize that planning is important. Leadership from the CEO is the best way to ensure such recognition.

2. The process should be open and accessible to those who have a legitimate need to participate. At the same time, it should be decisive. After listening carefully to all comments, the CEO should promptly make decisions and state openly the basis for the decisions. Failure to do so, whether on matters of procedure or of substance, will reward those who want to avoid the tough questions.

3. Draw up an ambitious schedule, and then forgive a little slippage, if necessary, as long as the planning process focuses productively on the main issues.

4. Remain flexible and be prepared to modify the planning procedure as you learn from your experience. Your subordinates and associates

will admire your willingness to be adaptive, as long as you have good reasons for the changes.

5. Take steps to ensure that the best, most self-confident, most imaginative faculty, staff, students, and administrators are appointed to the planning committees. In strategic planning, there is no substitute for broad perspectives and openness to responsible change.

6. Staunch support from the university's governing board will enhance the prospects for success in strategic planning. The CEO will be able to provide more decisive leadership if he or she has the board's clear blessing.

7. Be brief and to the point in all written materials prepared for the planning process. This will encourage wide understanding of the process and broader participation in it. Verbose instructions and reports discourage participation by the best people and breed additional verbosity.

8. Realize that, in all probability, you will find it necessary to include in your final written documents rhetorical reassurances for various schools, disciplines, groups, or individuals who need soothing. Likewise, you will probably not be able to nudge the university far enough toward measurable objectives. Do not despair on either count: Perseverance and tenacity in future revisions can win changes in the desired directions.

9. Computer services are fundamental and must be taken into account in every section of the strategic plan. Integrate computer planning with program planning whenever possible. If you end up with a single, separate chapter on computing, you are probably heading in the wrong direction.

10. Consultants, if well chosen, can be useful. They should be experts who can explain, in dispassionate words, what strategic planning involves. They can help diagnose problems when these occur. They can reassure struggling participants that other universities are also doing strategic planning. They will fly home promptly (or back to their departments) if so instructed.

11. Have a talented planning staff, willing to work hard, whose positive reputation is already well established on campus. I have this kind of staff. Cultivate them and tell them often how much you need their creative contributions to the planning enterprise. If you are lucky, they will remain in the trenches to help with new planning initiatives. They might even offer to make comments and suggestions on how to improve book chapters like this one.

Reference

Keller, G. *Academic Strategy: The Management Revolution in Higher Education.* Baltimore, Md.: Johns Hopkins University Press, 1983.

Donald C. Swain is president of the University of Louisville.

Threats in the external environment, the arrival of a planning-oriented new president, and new regional reaccreditation criteria prompted West Texas State University to undertake a successful strategic planning venture.

West Texas State University

Ed D. Roach

When, on July 1, 1984, I became the seventh president of West Texas State University (WTSU), the university stood at a critical turn. Originally a normal school, subsequently a state college, and now a regional university, the institution had seen four presidents in the last eleven years. Several factors resulted in a decision to initiate strategic planning at WTSU: Enrollments were declining. State appropriations were shrinking. There was growing pressure for mission differentiation among the publicly supported institutions of higher education in Texas. Finally, the university was preparing for a ten-year reaffirmation of accreditation from the Southern Association of Colleges and Schools. Among the criteria to be met, reflecting the fact that higher education has entered a new era of assessment, was a requirement that an institution have in place a comprehensive planning process.

Shortly after my arrival, I began a strategic planning effort, convinced by my own background with planning that such an effort would greatly enhance the university's long-term vitality while responding to the Southern Association's expectations. The venture started in March 1985. It intended to examine every aspect of the university in order to develop strategic recommendations that allow the institution to attain future excellence. The work of the various planning committees benefited greatly from the reaccreditation self-study, completed in 1984, and the favorable report of the Southern Association's site visitors.

D. W. Steeples (ed.). *Successful Strategic Planning: Case Studies.*
New Directions for Higher Education, no. 64. San Francisco: Jossey-Bass, Winter 1988.

The Planning Process

Presidential Charge. Appointing a series of strategic planning committees early in 1985, I pointed out that higher education will face a continuing resource shortage and must become more output- or results-oriented. The university must identify the areas in which it could achieve a high level of excellence and then focus its efforts on them. The committees were instructed to address the reality of unstable, declining resources as they considered how to accomplish the university's goals; they were told to be bold rather than timid, to take the lead on issues, and to be proactive rather than reactive.

Structure for Planning. Planning at West Texas State proceeded in three stages. The first was the universitywide strategic stage, which involved an assessment of opportunities and threats in the external environment, consideration of institutional strengths and weaknesses, and the matching of these with institutional values, programs, and activities. The result was a series of recommendations as to mission, clientele, goals, program and service offerings and priorities, geographic service area, and competitive advantage. There followed recommendations as to programs and services to be developed, enhanced, maintained, reduced, and eliminated.

The measurement of institutional strengths and weaknesses was the most emotion-charged part of this stage of planning. To assist it, planners devised a matrix with which to match programs with such internal elements as faculty quality, centrality to mission, service role, and support equipment; to external factors, including demand by majors, demand for graduates, locational and comparative advantages; to potential public impact; to cost-revenue relationships; and to decisions on target goals.

The second stage of planning dealt primarily with implementation of strategic decisions. It proceeded through completion of plans for the financial, facilities, organizational, human resources development, and enrollment, admissions, and recruitment areas. It framed specific goals in each area.

Planning committees for both the strategic and implementation stages contained members from various university constituencies, including general administration, department heads, faculty, and students. Faculty members were selected on the basis of peer regard for teaching or scholarship, conceptual abilities, emotional maturity, and demographic diversity. The strategic decision committee, chaired by a dean, contained fourteen members. The implementation committees numbered six to seven members each.

The third stage of the process was unit-level planning. Each college and administrative support unit devised a plan, within the boundaries of the universitywide strategic and implementation plans, stating unit mission, goals, and priorities for the next three to five years. Completed unit plans received review and evaluation from the university standing committee on planning. Budget decisions followed, based on agreed-on priorities in the unit plans.

Process for Regularized Review. Strategic planning is essentially a way of thinking. It is not a separate activity but an integral part of the overall process of managing. It should focus consistently on decision making. Because strategic planning is a continuous process, it is important to provide for systematic revision and reevaluation. The environment, internal strengths and weaknesses, and institutional values all change. An organization must, therefore, continuously assess its key decision areas.

West Texas State created a standing planning committee to perform regularized review. Activated annually by the president and charged to develop what eventually will be a five-year rolling plan, the body also appraises the entire planning process. The review considers whether there should be changes in the basic framework for planning or in the size and composition of the planning committee, what the respective roles of the administration and faculty should be in the planning process, and whether there should be improvements in the coordination and integration of the various stages of planning. It also looks at whether adequate data are being developed, whether there is appropriate staff support for the planning process, and whether the planning process overall is functioning as it should, especially in terms of the involvement of the key decision makers with the larger campus community.

Time Frame and Central Theme. The first two stages of planning consumed fifteen months and required participation from the entire university community. Assuming that higher education had ceased to be a growth industry, especially in WTSU's service area, planners concentrated on building on institutional strengths and on doing fewer things but doing them well.

Turbulent External Environment. A major external factor heightened the organizational disequilibrium and uncertainty accompanying the planning process. Paradoxically, constructive change proceeds best under conditions of relative stability. Texas, however, had become overly dependent on its petroleum resource and was unprepared for the precipitous decline of oil prices that began toward the end of 1984. In a fifteen-month period between 1984 and 1986, WTSU's planning period, oil prices fell from roughly $33 per barrel to as low as $10. For each $1 decline, state revenues shrank an estimated $100 million. The falling state revenue base compounded the uncertainty resulting from the major organizational changes that followed university planning efforts.

The Completed Plan

There are many effective planning approaches, but, to be successful, the approach must fit the unique needs of a particular institution. West Texas State University's plan contained several major sections when it was completed.

Mission Statement. A reexamination of the mission statement began early in the strategic stage of planning. A revised statement resulted, moving the university from open to selective admissions. The institution remains committed to the primary aim of serving students. Its foundation is a broad, general education to equip students for lifelong learning. To this foundation are added the goals of providing quality teacher training, preprofessional and professional education, and education in the arts.

Goals. The plan defined twelve institutionwide goals, which were refinements of the priorities identified in the first two stages of planning activity. These goals drew on the university's mission, its administrative and leadership style, and its form of governance. The chief goals included:

- Implementing appropriately selective admission requirements and student retention programs
- Enhancing the quality of student campus life
- Establishing a venture fund to encourage academic innovation
- Developing an institutional advancement program able to provide the margin of difference between state funding and the level of excellence to which the university aspires
- Improving campus space usage, facilities, and appearance
- Achieving faculty salaries comparable to those of peer institutions
- Developing students' basic skills, including economic and computer literacy.

University Organizational Plan. Perhaps the most controversial and difficult question facing planners was how to organize the university. The institution, with 6,000 students, employed a traditional structure that would have worked well with 15,000. Analysis revealed that very small organizational units could produce inefficiency, and larger ones could produce problems with span of control. The Texas state funding formula forced careful consideration of the size and number of units and dictated, in turn, creating fewer units while increasing the units' coherence and efficiency.

The organization committee examined several possible goals of reorganization before presenting the president with two models. Potential goals included diversion of funds from administrative to academic uses, clarification of administrative roles, balancing emphasis areas with school or college size, gaining disciplinary coherence, streamlining the curriculum, enhancing collegiality, and allowing WTSU to deal with educational trends advantageously. Discussion referred to mission, resources, demand, accreditation requirements, and the like. One model proposed a structure consisting of a College of Arts and Sciences and a College of Professional Studies, each with several large divisions. The other proposed a four-college structure in which the professional areas would be mixed with various components of arts and sciences. The committee noted the advantages and disadvantages of each model.

On the premise that form should follow function, I chose the second model, as it promised the best fit between structure and institutional mission. The most painful and traumatic of the university's planning decisions, this decision replaced seven colleges and twenty-three departments with four colleges and fourteen departments.

Academic Priorities. The need to do fewer things but to do them well required the prioritization of academic programs so that the university could concentrate its resources and achieve its primary goal of attaining excellence in all of its endeavors. The final plan drew on recommendations of the strategic decision committee, the reaccreditation site visitors, and members of the president's staff in determining which programs were to be added, enhanced, maintained, reduced, or eliminated. Low enrollment and inability to preserve desired quality while being reasonably cost efficient were the chief reasons for eliminations or reductions. Our research had shown that maintenance of small programs entails real added costs by spreading resources thinly and diluting quality. The vice-president for academic affairs accordingly launched an ongoing evaluation process with target graduate and undergraduate student-faculty ratios for each program and required review of any program that fails to maintain the target ratio after a reasonable time. The process created, in effect, a "sunset law" for academic programs, recognizing that while enrollment is not by itself a sufficient measure of quality, neither is it irrelevant.

The monitoring of staffing levels will also help to achieve the goal of competitive salaries for faculty, as it provides a means for allocating and reallocating resources among programs and associated faculty.

Administrative Priorities. Proceeding through an analysis like that used to set academic priorities, the plan recommended additions, enhancements, maintenance, reductions, and eliminations of administrative offices. Many changes in administration resulted.

Intercollegiate Athletics. Believing that the university should compete athletically at a level in keeping with its mission as a regional institution and with its goal to achieve excellence while reducing expenditures for sports, I recommended withdrawal from the National Collegiate Athletic Association (NCAA) Division I Missouri Valley Conference and affiliation with the Division II Lone Star Conference. The regents approved the proposal in February 1985.

Both strategic planning and the new conference membership invited a review of the role and direction of intercollegiate athletics at WTSU. A newly recruited athletics director, charged with the responsibility to do so, led the way in assessing the direction of and in setting goals for the athletics program. Three goals were stated: the recruitment of good *student*-athletes, effective competition for conference championships, and attainment of regional and national recognition through winning berths in Division II play-offs. Meanwhile, the move to Division II, which required competition in only four men's and four women's sports (instead of eight in Division I) allowed a reduction in the number of intercollegiate teams and a concentration of resources for more effective competition in the remaining sports.

Following a review that considered centrality of the athletics program to WTSU's mission, potential for a quality team, spectator interest, and cost effectiveness, the university eliminated men's and women's cross country, indoor and outdoor track, and men's golf. The resulting annual savings were $94,000. The redefined athletics program preserved the priority of the academic enterprise while allowing athletic competition at a level that will maintain student pride and win appropriate regional and national acclaim.

Human Implications and Timetable for Implementation. The regents approved reorganization in May 1986, and as many of the required changes as possible were implemented by September 1. The administration acted to lessen the negative impact of reorganization on personnel. Normal attrition and reassignment of duties where feasible accomplished virtually all personnel reductions. Individual counseling was provided to affected persons, and every reasonable effort was made to ease the impact of the plan's implementation on faculty, staff, administrators, and students.

Enrollment, Admissions, and Recruitment Plans. Given declining enrollment and decreasing state funding, the shift from open to selective admissions was risky. Nevertheless, it has served the university's mission and goals, enhancing the institutional image and allowing us to devise a marketing plan and a retention program.

Human Resources Development Plan. Changes in mission and organization led to the identification of a number of faculty and staff development needs. The committee on human resources development accordingly framed recommendations concerning the development of faculty and administrative resources, the mix of teaching, research, and service and the faculty profile.

Facilities Plan. Too often, the facilities plan drives the academic plan. Strategic planning should result in an academic plan that shapes the facilities plan. The facilities committee was therefore charged to update the master facilities plan in line with the university's current mission and goals. The committees ultimately recommended three project phases, an action schedule, and a consulting contract with a firm specializing in campus architecture in order to develop a campus master plan based on the strategic plan.

Adopting a "stewardship" theme, the firm completed a highly innovative campus plan in February 1987. Far-reaching recommendations turned some major facilities problems into opportunities. A space surplus (the university had more than twice the educational space that the Texas Higher Education Coordinating Board's standards allowed) became the basis, in phase one, for mothballing unneeded areas, for replacing an antiquated student union on the campus periphery with a new one in a converted major central campus building, and for providing improved housing for certain academic units in the converted facility. Phase two will bring a new student union building and added green space to the heart of the campus, which will be closed to vehicular traffic. These steps will create a new focal point on campus, while closure of unneeded areas will offer savings on utilities, care, and maintenance costs. The completion of phase three will meet all facilities needs through the year 2000, serve the objectives of the strategic plan, and furnish a win-win situation to the students, the faculty, and the taxpayers of Texas.

Financial Implications. Program reductions and eliminations required by the strategic plan carried projected savings of almost $1 million. Almost all of these savings evaporated because the state legislature, meeting in special session in the summer of 1986 to grapple with the state's declining revenue base, reduced institutional budgets sharply. Without the flexibility gained through strategic planning, the university would have had no choice but to enter a state of financial exigency. Moreover, even though the budget cut prevented the intended immediate reallocation of savings to faculty salaries, planning allowed the identification of the gaps between present funding levels and those needed to bring about the desired level of excellence. This knowledge, in turn, helped the administration and the university foundation to plan aggressively for a capital campaign.

Unit-Level Planning. As stated earlier in this chapter, the four colleges and the administrative support units developed five-year plans containing their missions, goals, and priorities. After approval, these plans helped shape the university budget.

Implementation

Administrative follow-through is the key to successful implementation of a strategic plan. Budget decisions must be based on a careful review of approved unit plans. Presidential leadership in linking planning with budgeting is critical. Failure to maintain this linkage reinforces the widely held view that planning is an empty mental exercise unconnected with action. Administrative action plans, specifying actions to be taken, by whom, and when, can overcome the tendency to lose focus and engage in busywork or routine activity. WTSU also employed management by objectives: Division heads were instructed in how to develop "key result areas" with their personnel; these result areas were expressed in terms of measurable objectives negotiated between managers and their staffs. Use of this device and the action plans allowed tracking of progress and of individual assignments.

Observations

Presidential Leadership. Strategic planning may proceed through use of a committee with a majority drawn from the faculty, with the chief academic officer as chair and the president as final reviewer or coordinator; through use of a committee containing a large administrative membership with the president as chair; or through use of some other model. Local circumstances, traditions of governance, and needs will determine which model best fits a particular university or college and what level of presidential involvement will work best.

What is certain is that a strong presidential commitment to planning is essential for success, no matter which planning model is employed. Successful strategic planning illustrates the close connection between management, which aims to do things right, and leadership, which seeks to do the right things. The president, as manager and leader, must ensure that unit and institutional goals converge, and he or she must make planning an integral part of the institution's culture. This all takes time as well as ability; as Carnegie Mellon University President Richard Cyert recently remarked, it takes approximately five years for an idea to pervade a university.

Organizational Culture and the Process of Change. There are many obstacles to planning in higher education. Former University of California–Berkeley Chancellor Clark Kerr once observed, "There are two reasons why presidents don't like to plan. First, faculty don't like to plan. Second, presidents, by nature, are not masochistic." Further, planning involves assessment, which tends to make people uncomfortable. Beyond that, when resources are scarce, planning implies a reallocation, with some programs losing and others gaining. It is thus not surprising that strategic planning expert George Keller concluded that planning "does not take very well" in an already successful situation. Rather, a real or perceived external threat, new opportunities, or an ambition for greatness seem to be requisites for gaining support for strategic planning in higher education.

Put another way, strategic planning involves change, which threatens an institution's culture. It is not a venture for the faint of heart. It meets resistance, setbacks, difficulties. A well-designed process for planning can minimize obstacles. Recognition of the importance of getting started and of guarding against a paralyzing perfectionism can keep planning moving.

Presidents and others contemplating strategic planning need to be aware of another hazard, too. This is what Rosabeth Moss Kanter calls "the difficult middles." Because change is always disruptive in the short run, there is a tendency for everything to look like a failure at the midway point in a transition when disequilibrium is at its greatest. At this juncture, called by some the "valley of despair," critics, "come out of the walls," charging with some accuracy that performance was higher prior to change. Strategic planners must be willing to persist, to outlast the critics, until the expected results are obtained.

Planning and Communication. A college or university is by definition decentralized, collegial, and open. Strategic planning, however, addresses sensitive issues that often require confidential consideration. I recommend arriving at an early understanding with internal and external constituencies about how and when progress in planning will be reported. Releasing at certain points along the way "white papers" detailing the committees' progress can be very helpful in controlling rumors and providing needed information and reassurance.

Media relations constitute an important communications issue. Failing to anticipate high regional press and telecommunications interest in planning at West Texas State, the administration too often found it necessary to react to inquiries prompted by calls to the media from threatened individuals who urged an investigation, for example, of the plan to abandon a historic open-admissions mission. It would have been better actively to work with the media from the beginning, rather than waiting until late in the planning process to initiate contacts.

Conclusion

Strategic planning recognizes and emphasizes the fact that a college or university is a system. It is a system that acknowledges that faculty and facilities, students and staff, athletics and academics, custodians and cashiers all must work together in harmony to achieve institutional goals. Leadership furnishes the impetus and lubrication neccessary for successful planning within the system. Leadership must inspire and focus strategic planning in the college or university setting in a manner that recognizes the decentralized and collegial elements that are present in every institution of higher education. Presidential leadership must also ensure the continuation and improvement of the planning process after it is underway. Finally, the president must ensure that resources are actually allocated on the basis of the priorities established through strategic planning.

Despite how recently strategic planning was initiated at West Texas State University, results are already apparent. The need remains to strengthen linkages between planning and resources allocation and between planning and governance. The standing committee on planning is just beginning its review of unit plans. The planning process itself will soon be evaluated, as further iterations take place.

Meanwhile, there have been some significant gains:

1. The Texas Coordinating Board has praised the university for its space-saving plans, which include the first reductions submitted to the coordinating body in its twenty-two-year history.

2. A special 1987 legislative session that sharply increased taxes enacted a modest appropriation increase, which included funds dedicated to merit increases for faculty and staff at WTSU.

3. Plans for a capital campaign are advancing rapidly with assistance from a consulting firm and support from the executive committee of the university foundation, whose membership has tripled to seventy-five.

4. The university has received a $400,000 endowment for scholarships from the Mesa Petroleum Company.

5. Commitments have been received from the Mesa Petroleum Company and T. Boone Pickens, Jr., to endow the College of Business. The college now bears Pickens's name in recognition of this and his many other contributions to the university. The new college endowment will also support the salary of the person selected to be dean.

6. Four faculty development or sabbatical leaves (one per college), funded by the WTSU Foundation, were announced in the president's fall 1987 state-of-the-university address.

7. An endowed professorship in fine arts, announced in November 1987, represents the first step toward accomplishing the president's goal of establishing at least one such position in each academic department.

8. In spite of the rejection of 10 percent of the applicants, freshman enrollment was up 16 percent in fall 1987. The freshman average American College Testing (ACT) score was up a full point, to nearly 19 against a state average of 17.3.

9. Finally, the move to NCAA Division II athletics has been highly successful, both competitively and in terms of lowering costs. The university won conference championships in 1986–87 in football and in women's basketball, as well as a cochampionship in men's basketball. It was the only institution in the country to host regional play-offs in both men's and women's basketball. Attendance increased for both football and basketball, and the university's football team ranked twelfth nationally in Division II.

Strategic planning marked a significant beginning at West Texas State University. It has positioned the institution to chart its own course. Thoughtfully and courageously undertaken, it promises similar results to many other colleges and universities.

Ed D. Roach is professor of management and president of West Texas State University.

Strategic planning can successfully counter crises threatening a college's survival by clarifying the mission, by shaping institutional reorganization and curriculum development, and by focusing marketing efforts and attracting new support.

Westminster College of Salt Lake City

Douglas W. Steeples

Westminster began in 1875 as the college preparatory school of Salt Lake City's First Presbyterian Church. Antedating public schools, it originated in the same year as did Utah's territorial university. It was founded to educate Protestant youth in the Mormon Zion. Enrollment exceeded 200 in 1892, when the Utah Presbytery made it the nucleus of a new two-year college.

By 1974, when a covenant relationship replaced church ownership, the college had survived many challenges. These included a move from downtown to a suburban campus on Emigration Creek; two name changes, the last to Westminster College; four years, 1909-1913, with no students; near closure when World War I and then later the Great Depression ravaged enrollments; and a turn to four-year instruction in 1944. Full accreditation came in 1950. Westminster added to its Presbyterian ties loose association with the United Methodists and the United Church of Christ, but it received negligible financial support from these religious bodies.

Growing enrollment and federal aid programs had allowed the erection of fourteen buildings on a twenty-seven-acre campus by the time of independence. Westminster in 1974 had two new dormitories, a new nursing-science complex, a "basic but adequate" library, a modest admin-

D. W. Steeples (ed.). *Successful Strategic Planning: Case Studies.*
New Directions for Higher Education, no. 64. San Francisco: Jossey-Bass, Winter 1988.

istrative facility, ample teaching and athletics space, and a new student union. Endowment was only $400,000. The operating budget of $2.5 million depended on enrollment and tuition. Students numbered about 930 full-time equivalents (FTEs).

Westminster was the only independent college in the Utah-Wyoming area. It was unique, too, in being beyond the influence of the dominant regional church. It filled a special niche, through open admissions offering students sound, personalized instruction, and a community typical of small schools. Faith, sacrifice, and a clear mission as a private liberal arts college that emphasized some careers, such as teaching, assisted its survival through a difficult first century.

Crisis Background

The crisis that came in 1978–79, while rooted in Westminster's longer history, grew mainly from problems of the 1970s.

Precarious Finances. College finances were always shaky, with cumulative operating deficits a problem from the 1940s onward. Even in the sixties, when growth brought several new buildings, compounding deficits forced a retrenchment.

Poor Controls. Westminster lacked adequate financial controls. There were no departmental monthly and yearly comparisons of performance to budget, monthly cash flow projections, satisfactory journal entries, or sufficient detail on cash and bank transactions, payables, and receivables. Budget categories were too broad to be useful. As much as $600,000 may have disappeared with the hasty adoption of flawed computer accounting programs, implemented without backup. It was impossible until 1981 to discover that a 1975 centennial campaign thought to have raised $2.5 million returned but $1 million. Fieldwork for annual audits took up to five months in 1979 and again in 1980.

Poor Academic Records. Academic records were no better. There was no linkage of student registrations to billings; some students completed degrees while paying no tuition. Changing student course loads showing important shifts in enrollment patterns were untracked. The computer stored only the most recent two semesters of academic data. Faculty personnel files were fragmentary, outdated. There was no official record of faculty proceedings or the curriculum (except as a box of undated index cards).

Growth and Change. Inadequate information systems precluded effectively managing the growth of the 1970s. The decade preceding 1978–79 added a new nursing degree, majors in geology and aviation, an early childhood major and a master's degree enacting a deepened commitment to teacher education, and, after 1974, a mushrooming Alternative Entry Program (AEP). The AEP offered adults credit through rigorous portfolio assessment and through evening classes both on and off campus. Westminster had shifted from the liberal arts toward career preparation and adult students, without fully grasping what was happening. The faculty had grown from thirty-four to sixty, but liberal arts instructors only from twenty-seven to thirty-four. Nursing staff numbered twelve; education, nine; business, five. Student headcount rose 72 percent, from 849 in 1968–69 to a 1977–78 high of 1,464. Full-time and part-time student numbers gained respectively from 746 and 103 to 983 and 481.

Operating expenses, meanwhile, outran enrollment and inflation, rising 351 percent, from $1.335 to $4.742 million. Because Westminster often raised tuition in alternate years, it relied on growing enrollments to meet budget.

To the Brink. When Helmut Hoffman became president in 1976, he knew that continuing enrollment growth required expanding career-related and adult programs. He was shocked to find that the college had suffered two consecutive operating deficits, of $31,000 and $374,000. He could not know how shaky the situation actually was, given the state of college records. There was no margin: Unmet past obligations and current liabilities meant trouble if enrollment failed to rise enough to generate adequate tuition income. Deficits reached $495,000 in 1976–77, and $429,000 in 1977–78 when enrollment peaked. The student headcount fell the next year, to 1,432, and FTEs from 1,132, bringing the fifth consecutive operating loss and the seventh in ten years. Its cash reserves exhausted, the college covered losses with sizable bank overdrafts, a $600,000 bank loan secured by 80 percent of its endowment, and interfund borrowing of $650,000.

Adequate management information might have shown how the college had changed, helping it to avert the crisis. Faculty and staff increases of 75 and 80 percent outstripped enrollment advances of the decade. "General Administrative and Institutional Expense" had risen from $153,000 to $1.165 million. The 415 AEP students had driven enrollment growth, but suspicious liberal arts faculty in 1978 cut the top allowable credit awards to them from ninety-four hours from all sources (transfer, military, experience) to forty hours, only half of which could be experience-based. That half needed approval from unsympathetic academic departments, rather than trained evaluators. Their program dismantled, AEP students dwindled in two years, to 350, then 288. Westminster meanwhile was so underenrolled and underpriced relative to expenses that it needed to raise forty to forty-eight cents in gifts for every operating dollar spent.

Financial Exigency

Events forced the trustees to act at a special meeting on January 26, 1979. By late December, it was reported, revenue shortfalls had shown that "the college could not, perhaps, continue as a going concern." A new deficit of $573,000 loomed, on top of cumulative losses of $1.328 million incurred over the past decade. While considering a proposed major retrenchment, trustees shared sharp exchanges asserting that inadequate board supervision had let the crisis come. Tellingly, only nineteen of thirty-two members were present at the crucial meeting.

The board accepted with regret the unrequested resignation of the president. It named as acting president for the balance of the academic year a former miner and union-organizer-become-executive, James E. Petersen, lent by the Kennecott Corporation through the influence of a trustee highly placed there. The trustees unanimously declared "a bona fide financial emergency as referred to in the college manual." They likewise approved the liquidation of certain assets to pay bills, pledged themselves to raise funds to mend affairs, and ordered retrenchment as the administration proposed. They began meeting monthly, while key committees met weekly.

Retrenchment. Retrenchment eliminated intercollegiate athletics and a physical education major, slashed student services, and pared support efforts, saving $570,000. Campus morale suffered, just as had public confidence in the college with the declaration of a financial emergency. Cuts, with accelerated fund raising, however, resulted in a $127,000 operating surplus at the end of the academic year. President "Pete" did much to restore campus morale. Although both the University of Utah and Brigham Young University expressed no interest in absorbing and thus saving the college and the state legislature declined to appropriate assistance, there was some good news. March brought a commitment of support from the Mormon church. President Nathan Eldon Tanner, convinced of the need for an "educational alternative" in Utah, became honorary chairman of a $3.5 million, one-year fund-raising campaign that the trustees formalized in August.

In later spring, philosopher-philanthropist Obert C. Tanner funded a series of luncheons for potential contributors, an Academy for Educational Development study of the college completed by Dr. Sidney Tickton, and consulting services by former United States Commissioner of Education Dr. Sterling M. McMurrin. "Pete" oversaw admissions, brought in a new chief development officer, and formed a marketing committee. In September, a presidential search closed with the selection of a seasoned fund raiser, C. David Cornell.

Toward a Strategy: The Tickton Report. Dr. Tickton reported in November 1979. He made eight recommendations, based on a study of demographic, economic, and market factors and of Westminster's strengths and weaknesses. The college should reply to Utah's expanding adult and flat eighteen-year-old populations by restating its current mission and becoming by 1985 a "career . . . and profession-oriented institution of high quality with a liberal arts core program," enrolling 2,000

FTE students, 60 percent of them adults. It should develop a distinctive academic program, perhaps creating an undergraduate international management major. It should affiliate with and hold academic control of externally funded ventures, such as the American Institute of Applied Politics (AIAP). It should secure proven administrators. It must raise $3.5 million in a year to restore assets and meet current needs. It should constitute a board of twenty-one trustees willing to devote a day a week to the college and to bear chief responsibility for soliciting funds. It must achieve adequate financial and managerial control. And it must mount a marketing effort supporting its mission and objectives.

The Tickton report departed from the usual model for strategic planning in that, although thoroughly grounded in research, it came from an outside expert, rather than an internal planning process. The report set only the goals for the college for the next few years, leaving to Westminster the important planning task of determining the means to be used. In any event, "business as usual" had to end. Westminster needed to shift from transactional leadership, which merely responded to changing affairs and worked within existing parameters of opinion, to transformational and strategic leadership, which would create new bases of support for sweeping change and take the initiative in matching external opportunities with institutional strengths, priorities, and mission. President Cornell quickly recruited new heads of admissions, business affairs, public relations, and academic affairs. He plunged into fund raising. Soon after taking office, he also formed a faculty task force to frame proposals enacting calendar changes and Tickton recommendations as to mission statement and curriculum.

Implementing Recommendations. When I arrived in the summer of 1980 as the new academic dean, I helped to focus the faculty task force's proposals. In September, the faculty overwhelmingly approved a new mission statement, cast along the lines of Tickton report. The faculty also adopted an early-semester calendar replacing the dropout-prone January interim with a May term. We tightened distribution requirements, increasing curricular coherence. I facilitated creation of a management information system and the college's first long-range plan. Faculty soon approved in principle a nontraditional degree program with a revitalized AEP. Simplification of academic administration replaced academic departments and divisions with a smaller number of "program committees" and "faculties," freeing three FTEs to teach.

The failure of tuition income to reach budget in the fall of 1980 forced faculty cuts that had been put off for more than a year. After adoption of guidelines assuring a faculty role and due process in retrenchment decisions, majors were dropped in music (the choir enrolled three), geology, and political science (replaced by the AIAP, whose affiliation with Westminster the president arranged).

The termination of appointments of seven out of fifty-one faculty hurt, even though, where possible, affected tenured persons were offered nonacademic posts. A minority of liberal arts faculty that had coalesced against the cutbacks of the 1960s vigorously opposed both retrenchment and academic reorganization. Despite noisy contention, 83 percent of the secret ballots cast favored sweeping revisions of the contractual chapter of the new, greatly improved *Faculty Handbook*.

Gains continued throughout the following year. A reported $27,000 surplus in the unrestricted portion of the 1980 operating budget helped win accreditation for the first time from the National League for Nurses and a Northwest Association of Colleges and Schools reaccreditation (contingent on improvement in Westminster's finances), both in December 1981. The college retired its bank debt. A consultant furnished its first marketing plan. The new business officer improved controls and shared in implementing a flat full-time tuition charge for twelve to sixteen (instead of fifteen to seventeen) hours at the fifteen-hour rate, enhancing income.

Continuing Problems. Progress was uneven. There was an $88,000 net deficit in 1980, despite the favorable result in the unrestricted portion of the operating budget. Record gift receipts of $1.4 million fell far short of the $3.5 million campaign goal. Internal borrowing had repaid the bank loans. Deficits followed again in 1981 and 1982. In November 1981, anxious trustees again pondered retrenchment. Administrators staved it off in confidential board meetings that, in December, created an ad hoc planning committee and ordered the preparation of several scenarios for the future, including plans for closure.

In February 1982, the board was persuaded to reject closure for the time being. "Pete" resumed the helm, following the resignation of President Cornell. Board spokespersons announced the change and an imminent major gift at a special faculty meeting on February 23. In March, still hoping for such a gift and aware of the urgent need for increased operating funds, the trustees rejected administration pleas to hike tuition by 10 percent in 1982–83. Instead, they gambled that a tuition freeze would draw students and raised compensation by 5 percent. During the usual tuition-dry summer cash crisis, a few active trustees helped prepare an emergency fund-raising brochure but did not bring in the large gift. They also added $125,000 in unfunded maintenance to the new year's budget.

Back to the Brink. Westminster again approached bankruptcy in the autumn of 1982. Enrollment failed to improve materially. Full-time students numbered 512; part time, 677; FTE, 868—not enough to provide a fiscal base for efficient operation at current staffing levels. Even with the most hopeful fund-raising projections, a deficit of $500,000 loomed. Although there remained a small core of loyal support, many traditional students and adult learners, trustees, and much of the community had lost confidence in the college. Plans to revitalize the AEP were stalled. Westminster's academic reputation, despite the efforts of a committed faculty who were among its greatest strengths, was undistinguished. Students enjoyed adequate library resources only because the University of Utah was nearby. The auditors had for two years warned that deficits, debts, and $3 million of structural modifications needed to comply with the fire code "indicated that the college may be unable to continue in existence." Deferred maintenance added $3 million more of unmet needs, and the tired appearance of the campus—accentuated by the 1982 closure of a dilapidated major building—undercut new admissions and enrollment management efforts. The Northwest Association, recognizing how precarious the college's position was, required annual financial reports. Interfund borrowing stood at $1.2 million, of which $740,000 was from the $1.25 million endowment, and the cumulative operating deficit was $1.75 million. Top administrators knew in September that, barring a miracle, Westminster would run out of money on April 28, 1983.

Toward a New Strategy

Marketing Considerations. In October, the president's staff began weekly meetings that extended through the remainder of 1982, considering all planning data collected since 1979 in order to frame a marketing strategy. The revised college mission statement, embodying the Tickton recommendations, remained a usable and sound statement of purpose, program direction, and types of students to be served. An assessment of internal strengths and weaknesses showed that, although Westminster's able faculty continued to offer good instruction under difficult conditions, a new retrenchment was essential to avert closure. A careful estimate of the external environment confirmed that such a step threatened to shatter what little confidence remained in the institution's future. Matching external and internal considerations, the staff eliminated options one by one and within two weeks confidentially concluded that the only hope lay in adding to retrenchment a bold set of further steps. These must place the institution on a sound operating footing, empower the curriculum and enlarge its appeal, energize the governing board, and capture the imagination of Westminster's several publics in such fashion as to reestablish confidence and thereby attract the students and financial support without which it could not survive.

The last hope for rescue through receipt of a major gift vanished on November 24. A letter arrived that day from an important local foundation granting, instead of endowment or a large operating subsidy, fifty new, four-year, $1,000 merit scholarships yearly, to make a total of 200. Like several trustees, who could easily have delivered the college from near bankruptcy to an endowed prosperity, the foundation must be shown that the college could succeed on its own.

At a special, closed, glum meeting of the board's executive committee on November 29, the president's staff reviewed the choices and asked permission to prepare a reorganization plan. Finally, the committee agreed with the past board chairman: "Why not? Nothing else has worked. This might."

Intensive Planning. Planning advanced vigorously during the following six weeks. It progressed in strict secrecy, for premature disclosure carried two major risks. The first was that the faculty might force prolonged debate on any proposal, delaying action until it was too late to save the college. The second was that disclosure would remove the element of dramatic surprise considered to be essential to capture the imagination of the public and rally enthusiasm for a renewed college.

During the hectic planning interim, four staff members visited the University of Charleston, West Virginia, which had successfully reorganized, and heard its president counsel that Westminster's situation was more desperate than his had been. He advised, "Plan to succeed, but be prepared to fail." At trustee direction, there followed conferences with attorneys and the state commissioner of higher education to explore questions of liability, contractual rights, due process, and whether to reincorporate or simply transform the corporation. Regard for creditors' rights ruled out a bankruptcy reorganization. There was conversation with the president of the University of Utah. He said that university absorption of the college would require a year of planning, effectively negating that option. Westminster, he added, most needed to attract full-time, traditional students. It should not become the University of Salt Lake City as some of its officers wished, for such a name change could imply rivalry with the university. There were also meetings with marketing and advertising specialists.

Reorganizing Strategically

Adopting the Plan. On January 5, in morning and evening sessions, the executive committee of the trustees accepted the reorganization plan. Still maintaining secrecy, committee members then conferred individually with the entire board membership prior to a special meeting set for noon, January 17.

Gathering on January 17, the board elected a new chair and heard administrators summarize the plan. It then unanimously adopted five resolutions embodying the design. The first reaffirmed the existence of a state of financial exigency, in order to establish a basis for action. The second held that corporate transformation promised to end exigency. Through an eight-page amendment, it rewrote the articles of incorporation, changing the college's name and increasing board flexibility by transferring most regulations to the bylaws. The third required registration of the amended articles with Utah's secretary of state. The fourth, through a single, twenty-page amendment, rewrote the bylaws. Corporate employees and students lost membership on the board. A limitation of two consecutive, three-year terms assured membership renewal. A new "necessary and proper clause" enlarged board capacity for action. Creation of a national board of advisers was to improve fund raising. The executive committee headed a simplified committee structure and could act for the board between its meetings, now cut to three yearly. The intent was to fashion a more effective governing body.

A fifth resolution proceeded from the first four and directed the internal reorganization of the college. Administration was to be streamlined into three functional areas: education, support, and marketing. The academic program and faculty were to be reassessed and pared. Four schools would house a new curriculum: arts and science, nursing and health sciences, business, and professional studies. The last might offer for adults a nontraditional degree, with intensive modular instruction, distribution requirements addressed to adult experience, and courses developed through student planning with faculty mentors. All employees must be notified that their positions would expire with the current college on June 30, 1983, and must be invited to apply for available posts in the transformed college to open on July 1. Additional clauses treated budget, public relations, and fund raising and ordered completion of all necessary steps before July 1.

Implementation. During a January 18 surprise convocation to proclaim reorganization, workers erected new campus signs identifying "Westminster College of Salt Lake City." A press conference followed at once. All employees that day received letters announcing that their positions would terminate on June 30. Valuing tenure and the protections of the *Faculty Handbook,* the administration wrote to faculty promising to continue tenure rights and eligibility for tenure of current faculty appointed to posts in the transformed college. It later extended preference to current employees and carefully followed *Faculty Handbook* procedures as to both termination for exigency and new appointments in order to protect faculty. New faculty added after reorganization were to be eligible for multiple-year, renewable appointments, rather than tenure, to provide both job security and institutional flexibility.

"Pete" immediately became acting president of the new college and designated his staff as acting subordinates. Three weeks later, after he had been named president and had interviewed candidates, he appointed current staff members as full officers. Meanwhile, on January 20, he ordered the implementation of reorganization, including a review of curriculum and of needs for faculty and staff. Concurrently, boards of lay advisers were formed for the new schools. Academic programs and staff received careful study and comparison with those of six other Rocky

Mountain private colleges. On February 14, the administration sent resulting proposals to the proper three faculty committees for response by
March 1, opening its files and membership to use by the committees.

Abolition of Tenure. On February 25, fearing failure, the board's executive committee suddenly abolished tenure and voted to add thirty-day
cancellation clauses to future faculty contracts. Administrators won res-
toration of annual faculty contracts after securing from the Northwest
Association's secretary a virtual promise of loss accreditation unless this
were done. Trustees were adamant about tenure, though, and as late as
June some still insisted on written proof that the thirty-day clause really
jeopardized accreditation.

Curriculum and Staffing. The administration's curriculum and staffing proposal went to the executive committee on March 14. Faculty
committee representatives challenged aspects of the plan at the meeting.
Members of the executive committee met three more times with faculty
groups, and also with students, finding wide support for reorganization,
before unanimously approving the proposal with changes to meet some
faculty and student wishes. Eight faculty positions were dropped, including tenured posts in education and history. Also pared were nonacademic
areas, except for student services where additions had barely restored
losses from the cuts of 1979.

After notices were posted for all available positions and applications
were received, interviews followed for candidates. The executive committee received recommendations for faculty appointments on April 4. Contracts were offered on April 21, after committee adoption of the new
Manual for Faculty, budget, new unfunded trustees' merit scholarships
without numerical limit, revised degree requirements contemplating
senior comprehensive examinations and capstone courses as well as a
new freshman writing program, and review of financial options should
a major gift still not materialize. By June 1, reorganization was well
advanced.

Results

The effects of reorganization soon became apparent.

Short-Run Problems. For a few months, Westminster still grappled
with severe difficulties. In mid June 1983, the Northwest Association's
Commission on Colleges voted to issue to Westminster an order to show
cause why it should not lose accreditation, given its unsolved financial
problems. Summer cash needs again summoned emergency borrowing.
In December, pursuing the complaint of a retrenched faculty member, an
investigative committee from the American Association of University
Professors (AAUP) visited the campus. The committee ultimately published a seriously flawed, prejudicial report that offered a seemingly pre-

determined recommendation to censure the college's administration for alleged disregard for tenure rights. The report preceded a 1985 vote to censure.

Long-Term Success. As 1983 ended, it was clear that economies, renewed public and campus confidence, and stronger marketing, achieved through strategic reorganization, had begun a turnaround. Fall headcount enrollment was up 5.5 percent, to 1,255. Full-time students had increased 3.5 percent, to 530; part time, 7 percent, to 725. The Northwest Association did not issue a "show cause" order. The year ended with an operating surplus of $503,000, assisted by record gift receipts of $1.57 million.

Progress has continued. In 1987, fall headcount enrollment reached a record 1,583, with full-time students numbering 705. Buoyed by continuing strong gift support as well as rising enrollments and tuition revenues, the college anticipated its fifth consecutive, substantial operating surplus. In mid 1988, repayment eliminated the cumulative operating deficit for the first time in some fifty years, and all but $150,000 of $900,000 borrowed from the endowment was repaid. The endowment itself reached $2.4 million. During the five years following reorganization, the operating budget rose 46 percent, to $7.74 million. Dependence on gifts to fund educational and general expenditures fell to 23 percent, as aggressive pricing advanced tuition from $122 to $173 per semester hour and enabled it to generate revenues meeting 72 percent of such expense.

The reorganization and retrenchment were so carefully executed that they prompted no legal challenges. The AAUP censure has not affected faculty recruiting. Instead, increases that have made salaries comparable to those at similar institutions have permitted the addition of strong new instructors. Seventy percent of the business faculty, for example, now hold the doctorate. Faculty work on a campus where gifts of more than $4 million have brought a new central steam plant, demolition of a closed building and construction of a new business school facility, and resources with which to erect a new fine arts center in the near future. An academic loan will soon finance restoration of the college's most historic structure and related work, essentially meeting all remaining deferred maintenance needs.

The arrival of Charles Dick as president in 1985 furthered Westminster's progress. An experienced chief executive, Dick quickly won statewide respect as an educational leader, continued to strengthen the board of trustees, and providing ongoing strong administrative direction. Through use of a consultant, he made further improvements in enrollment management and student recruiting. Consolidation of all enrollment functions, discerning market segmentation, recourse to sophisticated computerized mailings that precisely target prospect groups, and the merit scholarships have been vital tools in a continuing strategic emphasis on student quality. A by-invitation-only honors program limited to twenty-five new students per year, with minimum American College Testing (ACT) scores of 25, has also helped. In five years, the average ACT scores of entering freshmen have risen from 18.1 to 21.2, and Westminster for two years has been, for the first time, rejecting applicants. The college has won unprecedented academic credibility, and was included in *U.S. News's* fall, 1988 list of the nation's twenty-five strongest regional liberal arts colleges.

There have also been strategic changes of direction. The intended, distinct adult degree has not been implemented, as it has become apparent that nontraditional students prefer to share in the ordinary degree and campus programs. A nontraditional master's of management degree has yielded to a popular master's of business administration program that now enrolls some 200 students. The senior capstone course and comprehensive examinations have been deferred, while a foreign language requirement has been introduced and music is being restored. But Westminster continues, in the main, along the strategic lines that have evolved since 1979, attracting a mix of traditional and adult students to a program that combines career preparation with the liberal arts and with very high quality teaching.

Conclusion

Westminster's experience illustrates important characteristics of strategic planning. It shows how external threats or opportunities can work as potent incentives for strategic action. It points to the valuable contributions that consultants can make. It illustrates the close connection between strategic planning and action. It indicates how changing conditions require ongoing revision where planning is truly strategic. It emphasizes the focal role of strong administrators and the need to persist amid adversity. Most of all, it shows how strategic planning can be a powerful instrument for rescuing an institution from crisis.

Douglas W. Steeples is dean of the College of Liberal and Fine Arts at the University of Southern Colorado and has served as executive vice-president and academic dean at Westminster College, Utah.

The adoption and systematic use of planning guidelines and the pursuit of a disciplined strategy for implementation have provided the University of Miami with a powerful process for shaping its future.

The University of Miami

Edward T. Foote II

As the decade of the 1980s began, perhaps no major university in the United States faced more problems—or opportunities—than the University of Miami. Only fifty-four years old and already the largest private research university in the southeastern United States, Miami had travelled farther faster than most, and the potential seemed limitless.

Then began the series of wrenching social disruptions that rocked the Greater Miami area. During the 1980 riots in the Miami black ghetto of Liberty City following a prolonged controversy over the death of a black youth, twelve people died. In this same period, the international drug trade from Latin America quickened through Miami as the major point of North American importation.

President Jimmy Carter's decision to welcome Cuba's "Mariel refugees" brought 125,000 new residents to Miami in a few weeks, increasing the size of the community by more than 10 percent and tremendously increasing the pressures on social agencies. As we learned later, a small fraction of these newcomers were hardened criminals whom Cuban President Fidel Castro had transferred from his jails to the boats, causing a sudden spurt in crime that frightened Miamians and caught the fancy of the international press. These calamities would have sorely tested the most mature of metropolitan areas. In Miami, among the youngest of America's major cities, the combination was predictably disruptive. Disapproving commentary from elsewhere reached a crescendo in 1981

D. W. Steeples (ed.). *Successful Strategic Planning: Case Studies.*
New Directions for Higher Education, no. 64. San Francisco: Jossey-Bass, Winter 1988.

when *Time* magazine ran a major cover story on Miami entitled "Paradise Lost."

Disagreeing with some of my friends who thought that I should have my head examined, and for reasons that I hope will soon become apparent, I was honored in 1981 to become the fourth president of the University of Miami. Homeless refugees were still sleeping beneath highway bridges downtown, but I had become convinced—and I still am—that this presidency was among the most exciting of our generation. I believed that the university would have unique opportunities to become among the best anywhere and in relatively short order.

I had a lot to learn. Large institutional planning was not among whatever other modest qualifications I may have brought to my new job. As a backslid journalist, lawyer, teacher, and law dean, I had never studied strategic planning nor guided a major university. The largest organization that I had tried to lead was the School of Law at Washington University in St. Louis, a fine institution but of a scale so much smaller that planning was relatively easy.

The Need for Strategic Planning in Higher Education

As I contemplated my new association with a major private research university then composed of a full-time faculty of 1,400, a student body of 15,000, employees numbering 5,200, and a budget of several hundred million dollars, I sought help. What I discovered after reading everything I could find and consulting with colleagues around the country was not promising. Most colleges and universities did not seem to be doing the kind of tough-minded, precise strategic planning that seemed necessary for the University of Miami if it were to prosper during such difficult years, although there were a few exceptions. I acknowledged our debt to a university planning pioneer, Richard Cyert, president of Carnegie Mellon, and to George Keller (1983), author of *Academic Strategy: The Management Revolution in American Higher Education*.

What I also found was that industry was light years ahead of universities in the quality of its planning. My colleagues and I discovered a wealth of information in American and Japanese business practices. That business should plan better than universities is not surprising. In a business organization, most of the power flows from the top down, from the board through the chief executive officer to other senior officers. The "bottom line" is profitability for the stockholders, which is easy to quantify and measure if not always to create. Centralized authority provides a natural condition for centralized planning.

Universities, on the other hand, are different creatures. Power is shared among the board, the president, senior administrators, and the faculty, even students in some cases. Universities exist not to make widgets or profits: Their central mission is to free individuals, faculty and students, to learn. Their "product" is ideas, which are impossible to quantify and measure. The intellectual individualism that is central to a university's existence is seemingly at odds with centralized planning, at least academic planning. This argument recurs frequently in the more theoretical phases of university planning debates.

In a theoretical ideal world, of course, there would be no need for university strategic planning. It *does* tend to cramp some styles. But in such a world, there would be as many books, laboratories, computers, and discretionary dollars as students and faculties might need. There would be no tuition, no politics, and no need for state legislatures or the federal government. There would be plenty of parking for all.

Fortunately, none of us in higher education lives in such a dull world. The University of Miami, I quickly found, was not at all dull in this respect. Not only were university resources strapped, but Greater Miami's "problems" had resulted in an enrollment shortfall during my first weeks as president that required a $5 million emergency budget cut.

Two Basic Approaches to University Planning

Because there are not enough resources to support the limitless needs of students and professors and there never will be, universities are confronted with two basic planning alternatives or variations on them.

Decentralized Planning. The first and most prevalent approach in American higher education is a vastly decentralized, often politicized system of squeaky-wheel planning and budgeting. Inertia in such a system is frequently the dominant force. Money often flows down the paths of least resistance, not necessarily greatest need. If a program exists, then of course it should; otherwise it would not. Woe betide the planner who suggests that, just because a school has lost a third of its students because of changing interests, its faculty should be shrunk in equivalent proportion. Shame on any Philistine who presumes to suggest that providing more books for undergraduates (not to mention fixing an air-conditioning system) may be more important than replacing a departed specialist in eighteenth-century literature, the Department of English being already half again as big as its sister departments at comparable institutions.

Responsive Centralized Planning. The second planning approach is some kind of centralized system that preserves appropriate academic priorities. My colleagues and I wrestled to strike the proper balance in our planning between the individual needs of faculty members, students, departments, and school, on the one hand, and the entire university, on the other. We sought, in other words, to adapt accepted planning principles to the special needs of universities. Our system evolved to include the advantages of both planning principles to the special needs of universities. Our system evolved to include the advantages of both planning from the bottom up—that is, from the faculties of the university's fourteen colleges and schools—and from top down—that is, from the central university officers.

The bottom-up planning occurs school by school, unit by unit, and program by program. This part of the planning reflects the individual and small-group aspirations of faculty members and students. The top-down planning brings to the process an ordering of universitywide priorities, institutional support, including the data necessary for the entire process to work and as much broad vision about the overall direction of the university as possible, in addition to the inevitable sobering fiscal realities.

Defining the Planning Process at the University of Miami

We sought to define real academic priorities, recognize real strengths and weaknesses, and shape not only plans but also realistic strategies for achieving them. Now in its fifth year, our planning process has served us well. It is still evolving, as doubtless it always will.

The essential first inquiry was: Who plans? Next and related was: What power do the planners have? In the early stages of our planning, finding answers to these questions occupied much of our time. There are many possible answers, reporting relationships, and power models. At some universities, separate planning offices exist. At others, administrators and faculty members are chosen from throughout the university to propose plans to ultimate decision makers.

Who Plans. After much discussion, we decided that the long-range planning committee should consist of the president (chair), the provost and the deans, the vice-presidents, and other senior officers of the university and elected representatives of the faculty. The committee now numbers thirty-eight. The associate vice-president for information resources and planning acts as both provider of information and secretary to the committee.

Advisory Power Only. The committee, as such, has no power except to advise the president. The power to make decisions remains as previously distributed, whether in the faculty and/or the admistration, or ultimately in the board of trustees. Having the leaders of the university guide the planning, but not the execution, works for us. Thus, a dean, as a member of the planning committee, is only an adviser but, as the leader of his or her faculty, is responsible for executing his or her part of the strategic plan. Planners are requested to consider each issue from the perspective of the university's priorities, not parochially. There are other opportunities for deans to argue for their schools, vice-presidents for their divisions.

Planning Committee Meetings and Functions. The committee meets several hours monthly, more frequently as necessary. Agendas tend to be short with broad topics to stimulate wide-ranging debate on large issues. Examples are major changes in systems of budgeting or governance; a new cost allocation system; proposed new schools, programs, or important academic directions; a significant new effort requiring wide understanding and careful coordination, such as our $400 million capital campaign.

In addition, planning committee meetings often include time simply to exchange information, clear the air, share new ideas or projects, brainstorm aimlessly, or seek help.

We encourage robust, blunt debate. We try to focus on the largest university issues. We challenge each other to question existing practices, make them better, sometimes discard them. Especially when there are differences of opinion, we try to have them fully aired in front of those who must make the final decision, so that the nuances of positions, as well as their conclusions, become apparent.

The long-range planning committee has no staff or standing subcommittees, although the president occasionally will appoint ad hoc committees to perform particular tasks and report back to the entire committee, then dissolve. Minutes are brief and general, the idea being to keep track of what subjects have been covered but not to displace or overshadow existing groups or individuals empowered to make decisions. Thus, we may consider generally the creation of a new school or program, but the ultimate work will fall to the appropriate faculties and administrators.

Guidelines for Establishing Academic Priorities

Early on, we debated and accepted "Guidelines for Establishing Academic Priorities." These have become exceptionally important to our work, even more so than we first imagined. In effect, they are the criteria against which we try to measure all important decisions. Because they are so central to our planning, they are quoted in abbreviated, but verbatim, form in Exhibit 1. Using these guidelines, which have served us well, we examine every school and college in the university.

Strategic Planning at the University of Miami

Mission. We began planning five years ago by defining and writing the mission of each school and of the university. At first, this appeared to be an empty exercise. Everyone knows that universities exist to foster teaching, research, and related public service. Our friends from industry insisted that defining the mission was critical to achieving the result, so we forced ourselves to think hard about our actual obligations.

Exhibit 1. General Guidelines

Quality. What we do, we must do well. A central part of every decision will be determining the actual quality of whatever we do. How good is an existing program or how good is a proposed program likely to be, all things considered? If we don't have enough information, why not, and how can we get it? What do objective, independent observers say about it? If we don't have any such observers, how can we find them? How do we rank in accepted or professional rankings, if such exist?

We have no room, if we ever did, for so-so offerings. Recognizing that in any university there will be differing abilities and levels of performance among people and programs, the acceptable range [at Miami] must be high, very high.

Research. What distinguishes a university from other institutions of higher education is that its mission, in addition to teaching, includes research and communication of the results. Research should be broadly understood. It includes all of the systematic, creative, contributing, exploring, artistic, scientific, original thinking—and publication—that occurs throughout a university.

What is expected in the School of Medicine is not expected in the School of Music.

But the principle must be the same throughout the university. The principle, arising naturally from the mission of a university, is that a central part of every academic measurement, whether the performance of an individual faculty member of a department or a school, a proposed program or an existing one, is the quality and quantity of original thinking and its communication to relevant others. The communication might be by book or article, a play or equations communicated to only a small handful.

Graduate, as Well as Undergraduate, Emphasis. Graduate and professional studies are intertwined with research and publication. This emphasis on graduate (and professional) studies should not be understood as a de-emphasis of undergraduate studies.

Need. Regardless of other considerations, how badly is a program needed, and by whom? A community crisis may persuade us to meet a need with a program that would not otherwise be a high priority for us. We may emphasize a research project, marginal otherwise, because it is especially needed. Needs change. The need may be gone. Or the need may still be present, but other institutions may have developed to meet it as well or better—or cheaper than we can.

Durability. How long is a program likely to last, stay strong, and be characterized by quality? Is it a short-term fix, tempting but not that important? Is it a program neither needed nor appropriate for the university, but 'fundable'?

Synergism. If a proposed or existing program strengthens existing strength, or would make the whole greater than the sum of the parts in any way, that is good.

Critical Mass. If we are to do it, do we have enough resources to do it at an acceptable level of quality? Have we reached that critical mass or not?

Whatever that critical mass is, a top priority must be to reach it. Thus, if any self-respecting history department at a major university of our size would have at least ten members and ours had eight, then we should build the history department to ten members as quickly as possible. But if we already had twenty historians, recruiting history professors drops to a lower priority, other things being equal.

How Much Does It Cost? Regrettably, we must pay our bills, among other boring necessities. Thus, if a program makes money, that's an advantage. If it loses money, that's a problem.

Exhibit 1. *(continued)*

If It Ain't Broke, Don't Fix It. We should not waste time debating what is decided or too obvious to require extensive elaboration.

(But be sure it ain't a.k.a., "The Emperor's Clothes Management Maxim.") The fact that a condition has existed for a long time does not suggest we should accept it as is. The existence of a perception does not ensure its validity. We must take such time as may be necessary to proceed toward decisions rationally, assessing reality, not folklore. We must acknowledge change.

Programmatic Guidelines

Must a University Do It? Is the program essential, part of the core 'universe' of knowledge? This essence includes the sciences, natural and social, the humanities and the arts, at least. Knowledge grows. What were recognized disciplines and high priorities in the past may be no longer. Genetic research is revolutionizing the natural sciences. The nature and names of disciplines change to reflect changes. Administrative structures change. Knowledgeable people may differ about whether a particular course or subspecialty is "essential," but general consensus about a core of human knowledge and disciplines does exist. Therefore, these should be adequately represented on our faculty. We must remind ourselves frequently as we plan what *must* be nurtured.

Should a University Do It? Is the program teaching, research, or a service directly related to high learning? If not, we shouldn't do it, unless there is a compelling community or social reason to do so for a limited period of time.

If Not Essential, Should the University of Miami Do It? For example, obviously medical education is not essential, but it is appropriate for a university to offer. It is appropriate that a school of medicine exists here. Schools of dentistry or agriculture are also appropriate for a university to have. I doubt that the University of Miami should have them.

If the proposed program, then, is not essential to the work of any university, the purpose, nature, and substance of the proposed program must be carefully examined to determine whether it should exist at the University of Miami. The "General Guidelines," summarized above, should be helpful in assessing all programs. We must also not only lead from our strength, but meet special obligations that come with our territory.

Special Characteristics of Location (examples only)

- The subtropics
- Unique or special Florida characteristics, such as the Everglades
- Proximity to the Atlantic Ocean
- Proximity to the Carribean
- Proximity to the nations of the Carribean, Central America, and South America
- Location in a "global" city of increasing international importance

Special Characteristics of Greater Miami (examples only)

- Multiethnic population
- Older population
- Rapid growth
- Leading port
- Tourism
- Center of international commerce and banking

Exhibit 1. *(continued)*

These special characteristics present both advantages and disadvantages. The point is that we should keep them in mind. Thus, our older population may be disinclined to vote for tax increases—a disadvantage to public services or education—but may present the advantages of opportunities. The University of Miami should be a major center of gerontological research. Our continuing studies courses should find markets among older people who live nearby.

Application of the Guidelines

These are guidelines, not inflexible rules. They are to guide us toward, not frustrate, wise decisions.

Some of the principles embodied in the guidelines are more important than others. Quality, for example, is well worth some seemingly wasted time in occasionally debating what "ain't broke." We should not artificially quantify the degree to which a program falls within each guideline, then add the results to find the answer. On the other hand, the guidelines are not just words. The fewer the guidelines that fit a program, the bleaker its future here. No matter how brilliant the idea, if its implementation would bankrupt the university, we cannot do it (although we should stretch far to try). No matter how brilliant the fund-raising scheme, if it is not something we should do, we will not do it. Inevitably, there will be leaps of professional judgment, even faith, bridging those gaps in our understanding that inevitably remain. We will take those leaps.

"No great human institution has been built timidly."

School by school, and throughout the university, we found that the mission was not quite as clear as we had at first supposed. What had been the mission of a given school a decade earlier may not have been any longer. The world had changed. We had changed. The emergence of Florida International University across town, for example, required a thorough reexamination of the missions of our schools of education and nursing. In the case of education, we have eliminated the undergraduate degree, requiring instead a major in arts and sciences together with a minimum number of courses for a Florida teaching certificate, and much greater emphasis on graduate work. In the case of the School of Nursing, we also moved to a primarily graduate orientation, reconstituted the faculty toward research, and physically moved the school from the Coral Gables campus to the medical center.

In the case of our School of Medicine, there is no local competition, but national trends and local demographics dictated refocusing a number of programs to meet such emerging problems as an aging population, the AIDS epidemic, and cancer research.

High Quality. With increasing competition from the state university system, we made a series of decisions to emphasize the highest possible quality. Chief among these was reducing the size of the undergraduate student body by 2,000 students. In effect, we cut off the bottom 20 percent of the class. The result has been a dramatic increase in high school grade-point averages and Scholastic Aptitude Test scores. The university is now repositioned in fact and perception as far more "selective" than formerly. We invested heavily in our honors program, which has grown from 200 to 1,300 students in five years. We created the first "residential college" system in the southeastern United States. Based on Ivy League models, this system creates living units within the larger university, integrating dormitory and eating facilities with classes, intramural sports, and other extracurricular activities, all presided over by a resident faculty master and his or her family, plus other faculty members who live there.

Finding unmet needs in our region, we created three new schools: architecture, communications, and international studies.

For each school and college and for the entire university, using the guidelines already quoted, we require critical inquiry into the following areas:

1. Mission.

2. The external environment—What is actually happening out there? In medicine, law, architecture, and so on, or in demographic trends, what realities must be taken into account as we plan? In our case, for example, we anticipated, but insufficiently, the impact of a Latin America debt crisis on our foreign student population.

3. Internal environment—What are our strengths and what are our weaknesses, honestly assessed?

4. Priorities—What is important? What is more important, and what is most important?

5. Goals—What do we intend to do next year and in the context of the next five years?

6. Action plans—Given the external and internal realities, our priorities, and our general goals, how, quite specifically, do we intend to implement those goals, and when?

7. Status of earlier action plans—How are we doing according to what we thought we should do?

8. The financial plan—How will we pay for it?

Our final strategic plan, several hundred pages long, includes separate plans for each of the schools, colleges, and divisions of the university, plus the central plan for the entire university, which reflects university-wide priorities. It includes a capital budgeting section.

Advantages of Planning. Advantages of this kind of planning system are several. Its openness promotes an honest exchange among the university's leaders and conversely minimizes rumors, posturing, and paranoia. It helps planners focus on the university's reality, rather than on untested perceptions. The process itself provides and improves relevant information. The university becomes more responsive to the real needs of students, faculty, and society. Decisions, especially controversial ones, achieve more credibility because of wide participation in their shaping.

Dreams—and plans—are cheap. The difference between just planning and strategic planning is the difference between dreaming and getting the job done. A plan without a strategy for implementation will not materialize. It is the disciplined system of continually creating such a strategy that is the essence of our task as planners.

Risks of Planning. No process for the resolution of human differences is perfect, and this kind of strategic planning holds dangers. Because we are so open and because most of our decisions among competing priorities are published for all to see, those prone to jealousy and bickering may be encouraged. Because the guidelines for making decisions are generally accepted by our university community and all concerned have an opportunity to join the debate, this has not been a problem for us. What is a problem is how much to publish, as some issues are confidential. Weaknesses or difficulties can be exacerbated by premature exposure. As the computers whir, there is the danger of too much blind faith in data and too little in the informed instinct of seasoned professionals. There is always the danger of too much orientation toward shifting markets and too little toward the essence of what a university must continue to do, regardless of the market forces.

The Need for Balance

In a sense, a properly functioning university, like a solar system, is an eternally adjusting balance between centrifugal and centripetal forces. The centrifugal forces are the myriad individual ideas and aspirations of students and faculty. Fortunately, these travel constantly in every conceivable and unpredictable direction. The centripetal forces are those that keep the institution intact for the benefit of each individual seeker. These include the mundane but essential services, from buildings and grounds to budgeting, as well as the preservation of those central standards and directions against which individual efforts are not only encouraged, but measured.

Strategic planning for the University of Miami, then, has become a systematic effort to maintain this balance of energies between the needs of each individual seeker and the needs of all seekers. If there is insufficient central pull—gravity, if you will—the planets will spin off untethered into the universe, but if there is too much, then the very essence of the university, the individual work of those students and faculty members, is destroyed by suffocating uniformity. Thus, like a solar system, strategic planning must constantly adjust. What is important is not one decision, one budget, but a process by which decisions are made in keeping with the fundamental principles of human learning.

Reference

Keller, G. *Academic Strategy: The Management Revolution in Higher Education.* Baltimore, Md.: Johns Hopkins University Press, 1983.

Edward T. Foote II is president of the University of Miami.

At Carnegie Mellon University, collaborative strategic planning promotes institutional distinction through the development of focused departments that exploit university strengths and opportunities.

Carnegie Mellon University

Richard M. Cyert

Strategic planning in universities has traditionally been an overlooked and underutilized resource. Most of the planning that has taken place in universities has been mechanical; it usually involves a simple model, a highly structured problem, and well-defined variables and output. In other words, it is what might be called deterministic planning, such as determining the impact on the number of classrooms and the furniture needed if enrollment were to increase by 5 percent. This kind of planning, while important, is not really interesting. In the great days of the 1960s and early 1970s, when students were available in large numbers, many universities had little need for strategic planning. Only the adverse and challenging circumstances of institutions encountering financial stress could prompt greater emphasis on strategic planning as well as on careful management.

On the other hand, strategic planning is far more important than mechanical planning for the long-run quality of the university. Strategic planning is necessary in order to identify the areas in which the university should be doing research and offering educational curricula, to specify the goals of the institution, and to determine the kind of university that is desired by the community. Further, the university must look at the world and decide where its students are going to go, and it must determine an educational program that is consistent with the kind of students that it wishes to attract and with the kinds of areas for which it wishes to

D. W. Steeples (ed.). *Successful Strategic Planning: Case Studies.*
New Directions for Higher Education, no. 64. San Francisco: Jossey-Bass, Winter 1988.   **91**

produce graduates. Thus, strategic planning is really a method for dealing with and making decisions about the basic nature of the institution.

Both determination of goals and the strategic planning process
depend on an analysis of the institution. Thus, we are dealing with a
system of simultaneous equations. Practically, the system is solved by a
process of trial and error. Goals are selected, and strategies are identified
to achieve those goals. When analysis determines that the goals cannot
be achieved, the strategy is changed or the goals are modified.

The Essence of Strategic Planning

Seeking a Distinctive Niche. The objective of strategic planning is to
establish a plan by which a department, college, or university can achieve
a position that gives it a special place among other departments, colleges,
or universities. The strategic plan should enable the particular academic
unit to achieve distinction in the areas that it decides to emphasize.
Thus, the organization must be able to specify a set of goals from which
a strategic plan can be formulated. The unit undertaking the planning
must determine what its advantages are compared to other departments,
colleges, or universities with which it is competing. Such advantages
may consist of possessing a desirable location or having a certain person
or group of persons on the faculty, or they may be based on the historical
traditions of the institution. Any institution has such strengths on which
to build and has characteristics that, if not unique, only a few other
institutions can match.

Analytical Ability and Comparative Advantage. A major comparative
advantage comes from the ability to analyze disciplines and determine
future directions. This process requires the judgment of experts in each
field and an ability to screen the analyses of the future. It also requires a
matching of the human resources, financial resources, and physical facilities available with those required by the new initiative.

This approach to finding a comparative advantage must be an integral part of any strategic planning effort. New areas of advantages cannot
be discovered on the spur of the moment, however. It is necessary to
build into the organization specific devices that will function, in part, as
antennae for the organization. One mechanism that has worked well at
Carnegie Mellon has been a series of lectures of distinguished scientists,
humanists, and practitioners. People are sought for these lectures who
have demonstrated an ability to sense future directions in their fields.
Lectures based on analyses and predictions of the future, followed by
small interdisciplinary group discussions, are the key to developing ideas.
As ideas are generated, methods for auditing their relevance and authen-
ticity are developed. Ultimately, this approach can lead to the development of a comparative advantage.

Uniqueness Is Essential. The aim of strategic planning is to place the unit in a distinctive position. Commercial marketing specialists refer to this objective as developing a "niche" in the market. The main point is that each college or university should look to its own strengths and weaknesses and try to develop its academic units to make the best use of their strengths. The worst action that an organization can take is to imitate another unit that it considers to be successful. Uniqueness is required if an institution is to establish a position for itself in the market.

Strategic Concentration of Resources

After a department has identified the areas in which it has a comparative advantage, it should try to concentrate its resources in those areas—for example, by hiring faculty members with appropriate specialties. The smaller the size of the department, the greater the need to concentrate resources. In this fashion, strength can be further developed, and the department attain a heightened level of excellence.

A department clearly needs to cover more areas in its teaching than simply those in which it is doing specialized research. In most fields, however, a faculty member who is a specialist in one area of research can teach in other areas, and thus, teaching requirements do not generally affect the principles of strategic planning.

Strategic Planning at Carnegie Mellon University

Strategic planning has been a major method for quality improvement at Carnegie Mellon University since 1972, when I became president. My first memorandum to the deans, written on May 22, 1972, shortly before I assumed office, proposed establishing a planning process. The memorandum, quoted here in part, laid out the basic philosophy of my administration. I have followed that philosophy for the past sixteen years.

The objective of our approach is to produce focused departments. As a small institution that wants to make a big impact, we must concentrate on the areas in which we can achieve a high level of excellence. My planning memorandum thus assigned a central role to the colleges and their academic departments:

> It has been clear to me for some time that this university needs an explicit statement of goals as well as a strategy for achieving them. I am hopeful that we can start the planning procedure as soon as possible. I have a number of ideas about the way in which this procedure might take place. This document is an attempt to summarize some of the ideas for your reactions with a view toward revising the document.
>
> The planning should take place, it seems to me, on a college basis.

There are several questions that we need to have answered by the planning. Some of these are the following:

1. Can this department achieve greater eminence without a significant increase in the number of faculty members?
2. In what specific areas in the field represented by the department does Carnegie Mellon have a comparative advantage? (This comparative advantage may come from the kinds of people in the department, or it may come from the existence of strength in a related department or from foresight in recognizing a new field in which we can get an early start.)
3. How would the composition of the faculty of the department have to change in order to achieve the goals of the department?
4. Are there "stars" in the fields that it would be critical to get in the department if we were to move?
5. What other areas in the department do we need to cover if we have only one or two in which we are going to concentrate?

I am sure there are other questions that can be raised. I would then see each department make its plans, and present them to the dean. I see the dean and perhaps the department heads and some other senior people attempting to evaluate and perhaps modify these plans. Ultimately, it would be desirable to [integrate] these plans into a plan for the college with an explicit statement of the goals of that college. [Plans should project costs, consider important problem areas for the next five years, and ponder interdisciplinary approaches.]

I envisage, then, that the plans for each of the colleges would be sent to all members of the policy committee. We would then take time to go over the plans for each college. Ultimately, then, the policy committee should decide the priority of the plans and with it some indication of the direction in which we should allocate our funds.

There are several keys to making our strategic planning effective.

Winning Support for Planning. It is first necessary to convince deans and department heads that strategic planning is necessary and will work as a way of improving quality in departments and colleges. At Carnegie Mellon, I estimate that it took about five years before the ideas of strategic planning permeated the university from the president through the deans and department heads and some of the senior faculty members. The natural tendency of department heads and faculty members is to try to build a department that is like every other department in the discipline, and, generally, a department wants to have someone representing each aspect of the discipline. It took a while to convince the department heads that it is possible to cover all the needed teaching areas while choosing faculty who could provide a strong concentration in particular research areas.

Continual Strategic Planning. A second key element is to recognize that strategic planning is a continual process. At Carnegie Mellon, planning takes place in a two-year cycle. Plans are developed in written form, are put together with other materials, such as the mission and goals statements of the university, and are published for distribution to faculty and trustees. The plans are ordinarily presented to the faculty over a period of three days. The trustees receive a description of the plans in a retreat, which is usually held out of town and which normally runs through a Friday, Saturday, and Sunday. The administration brings along the deans and faculty members needed to provide the required information. We seek to inform major constituents and win their commitment to the same set of goals as essential elements in the ongoing planning effort.

Integrating Planning and Budgeting. When the plans have been completed, we analyze the budgetary implications, and we hold detailed discussions with each administrator who has submitted plans in order to indicate which of the plans has been accepted, which has been postponed, and which has been rejected. The purpose of these conversations is to secure complete understanding, as well as to integrate the plans into the budgeting process.

Flexibility. We do not allow ourselves to become rigid in adherence to the plans. When opportunities arise with respect to ideas or to potential faculty members, we are prepared to make adjustments and move in a new direction in a particular department. In other words, planning is crucial, but it should not prevent an organization from being opportunistic. Having a plan does not mean that one can go to sleep between planning periods.

Value of the Planning Process. Finally, the planning process itself is in many respects more valuable to us than the plans. The process forces department heads, deans, and senior faculty members to look hard at their units and to ask how they can make improvements. We have learned that excellence, like freedom, can be achieved only at the cost of vigilance.

Some Examples at Carnegie Mellon

Psychology Department. Perhaps an ideal example of the application of these strategic principles has occurred in Carnegie Mellon's Psychology Department. For many years it attempted to cover the complete range of specialties in psychology (for example, clinical, industrial, experimental, and physiological), and, while it was a good department, it was not distinguished in any respect (in 1969, it was ranked thirty-fourth in the country). Through the strategic planning process, it became clear that a major potential strength of the department lay in the quality of our Department of Computer Science and its work on problem solving. The Psychology Department thus began to develop a concentration in cognitive psychology. With a few judicious appointments of new faculty members, the department quickly attained the leading position in the country in the cognitive area.

It was also decided that a comparative advantage lay in social psychology because of the relationship of the Psychology Department to the Graduate School of Industrial Administration, whose faculty included social psychologists with a strong interest in business applications. Developmental psychology, because of its links to both cognitive and social psychology, was the third area to be supported. Other specialties in the department were gradually phased out, and the description of the department in the university's catalogue was clarified so that students would not be misled. These changes and various faculty appointments were made in conjunction with the strategic plan. An average of the scores in the four categories of strength measured in the most recent survey shows the department to be tied with one other as the most highly regarded in the country.

Mathematics Department. Our Department of Mathematics had been solid for a number of years but had lost its central focus because of changes in faculty and administration. For some time, the department had been losing undergraduate majors. When the department head position became open, it was decided to make applied mathematics the department's major thrust, with the provisos that pure mathematicians would not be purged and that the department would not be allowed to become too narrow. In other words, the mixture within the department was to change according to a strategic plan. A new department head was brought in from an outstanding pure mathematics department. He came to Carnegie Mellon because he believed in the new strategy. The result has been a transformation of many aspects of the department. Morale is higher than ever before. The undergraduate applied mathematics program, as developed, has drawn a tremendous number of students. The Department of Mathematics has enjoyed the largest increase in undergraduate enrollment of any department in the College of Science, and the number and quality of graduate students have also improved. Most observers now rank the department among the best applied mathematics departments in the country, and it is getting stronger.

Transforming Departments Is Not Easy. I do not want to create the impression that it is easy to transform a department by simply developing and applying some elementary strategies. Selecting the appropriate areas to emphasize, determining the wisest departmental thrust, and stimulating change can be quite challenging.

Implementing Change

Implications of Decentralized University Organization. The university is a decentralized organization, and it must be managed as such. However, when a decentralized organization is run without any central leadership, difficulties arise. Therefore, the management of a university must achieve a balance.

One can make the argument that the university presidents have, in effect, been using the Japanese style of management for many years. Through the tenure system we are familiar with the concept of lifetime employment, and we recognize the need to secure consensus before making radical shifts. More important, we know that we must obtain input from the faculty before we take actions. The structure of a university has at times been called "organized anarchy." Although I do not quite agree with this characterization, it certainly captures some elements of the reality.

Thus, in attempting to develop strategies for departments through central leadership, one must work directly with the deans, the department heads, and the faculty. This situation resembles that in industry, where both top-down and bottom-up management approaches offer advantages in implementing plans.

Need for Centralized Leadership. The planning that works best is shaped to a great extent by the faculty in a department. However, no planning would take place at all without the discipline imposed on the organization from the central administration. Planning forces us to deal with an ambiguous future. Many faculty members are by nature averse to risk and have moved into academic life because they want certainty and security. So it is that the planning process must be initiated by the president, who must be actively interested in it and must participate fully in discussions.

Similarly, planning within a specific college of the university must be led by the dean and his or her department heads, who should involve at least their key faculty. Ultimately, the plans must be exhibited and then monitored, preferably by a universitywide long-range planning committee chaired by the president and including the university's major academic officers as well as the deans. As the strategic planning reports are completed, each dean reports to and gets feedback from the committee. Thus, he or she is able to make further revisions. Nonacademic units for which strategic planning is appropriate can be handled in the same way.

Completed plans should be presented to the faculty, students, and trustees. Responsibility for implementation rests with the administration, which must find the resources and provide the organizational structure for achieving the goals.

The weakness of this approach is that it follows traditional lines and makes radical action unlikely, although certainly not impossible. For example, with essentially this mode of operation, Carnegie Mellon University phased out a department and eliminated several programs.

Role of the President. There are other ways to organize the planning process, such as along program lines; however, any approach that operates outside the organizational units can become exceedingly awkward. The president must take the role of educator in the planning process. Part of his or her responsibility is to educate the deans and the department heads about the concepts of guiding the institution's strategy. Provision of feedback on the preliminary reports from department heads and deans is one means by which the president may accomplish this task.

Finally, after the planning reports are completed, the president must draft a statement of the overall goals of the institution. This statement becomes a kind of constitution, a guiding framework, for the operation of the university over a specific period, and it should be widely distributed to both faculty and trustees.

Richard M. Cyert is president of Carnegie Mellon University.

*In the newly competitive realm of higher education, strategic
planning offers a systematic method for defining colleges and
universities in order to enhance their strengths and market
positions and to shape their futures.*

Concluding Observations

Douglas W. Steeples

Edward Foote, writing about the University of Miami in Chapter Eight,
correctly observes that the need for institutions of higher education to
undertake strategic planning originates in the imperfect nature of our
world. Ours is a world that provides colleges and universities with
an insufficiency of resources—whether books, laboratories, or parking
places—but "limitless needs of students and professors." The tension
between needs and available resources, Foote humorously continues,
makes for a much more interesting world than a theoretical and ideal
one in which there are no problems.

A review of the chapters in this volume identifies an additional powerful incentive for the pursuit of strategic planning in academia. That
incentive, too, is rooted in the character—in this instance, in the
changed character—of the world of higher education. Demographic
changes have propelled American colleges and universities, like Alice,
into an unfamiliar new world, a world of swift change and unprecedented rivalry for students. Here, for a great many institutions, as Alice
was informed about the new country that she had entered, "it takes all
the running you can do to keep in the same place. If you want to get
somewhere else, you must run at least twice as fast as that!" (Carroll
[1872], 1982, p. 104). In short, colleges and universities have entered a
realm long familiar to business—the realm of competition. It is hardly
surprising that, under the circumstances, many of them have come to

D. W. Steeples (ed.). *Successful Strategic Planning: Case Studies.*
New Directions for Higher Education, no. 64. San Francisco: Jossey-Bass, Winter 1988.

embrace the concepts of strategic planning and management that first flourished in the business world.

The Focal Elements of Strategic Planning

Unlike earlier versions of planning in academia, which our writers have variously described as mechanical, deterministic, theoretical, and concerned to build mathematical models, strategic planning is practical, flexible, and action-oriented. It is, as Richard Cyert comments, "really a method for dealing with and making decisions about the basic nature of the institution," a method pursued to match educational programs with the kinds of students an institution seeks and the kind of world for which it wishes to prepare them.

While the precise method of decision making may vary in detail from one institution to another, there are elements common to all successful ventures in strategic planning. The foundation of all strategic planning lies in the development of a specific vision for an institution. This vision must comprehend the entire institution, and it must reflect decisions as to critical development paths in five areas:

- Mission, including specific conceptions of an institution's reason for existence, its unique characteristics, its intended constituencies, its geographic service area, its major program emphases, and its distinctive civic and service obligations
- Target audience, meaning which and how many students and in what sort of desired mix
- Program priorities and offerings, including any new initiatives as well as maintenance or modifications of existing programs
- Comparative advantage, encompassing the ways in which an institution builds on its singular strengths and differentiates itself from rivals so as to occupy a strategic market niche
- Key objectives to be pursued, containing an understanding of the material and human resources required to accomplish goals

The decisions in these five strategic areas must rest on careful analysis. An institution's internal strengths and weaknesses must be understood. The external environment must be continually examined for threats, opportunities, and important trends in the demographic, social, economic, educational, political, and legal realms. As Robert Lisensky notes, it is critically important to possess an articulated and wide-ranging information system that permits the identification of trends both inside and outside of the institution over a considerable period of time. And, finally, it is essential to match internal strengths with opportunities residing in the wider environment in order to define institutional goals that are realistic and attainable.

The planning process as described thus far reckons with the entire institution as the unit of analysis. The peculiarly decentralized character of colleges and universities requires a careful balancing of initiative from the institution's leadership with the individual aspirations of faculty and students. Richard Cyert writes that it took some five years of persistent effort for the ideas of strategic planning to permeate Carnegie Mellon University. Winning support, generally through a broadly participatory process involving the governing board and faculty, is crucial to the creation of a shared strategic vision.

Implementation of a vision is the next step, and one that also requires broad involvements. Operating units—academic and other departments, for example—must devise their own congruent strategies in order to connect an institutionwide strategic conception with ongoing operational plans. To allow for evaluation, prioritization, and subsequent assessment of progress, unit plans need to be specific, to state goals precisely, to stipulate time frames for the accomplishment of objectives, and to state resource requirements. After extensive consultation, unit plans are forwarded to the institution's central planning committee for approval and priority ranking.

University control systems ensure that there is coordinated effort toward implementing the plans. Budgeting, which allocates resources and accountabilities so as to encourage change in desired directions, is the most important control instrument. One means for implementing planning priorities is the use of a budgeting continuum. Where this expedient is employed, universities prioritize spending by determining which initiatives or programs are to receive how much support from regular operating funds, which from external funding, and which should receive no funding. David Gardner, as president of the University of Utah, used a comparable approach. Given limited resources, he considered it most advantageous to invest first in those strong areas where a prudent added expenditure would result in a program of genuine distinction. Next in priority were programs where a larger investment would yield an appreciable return in terms of improved quality and standing. Lowest priority was reserved for areas where a substantial added commitment would generate a much less considerable improvement. The use of a 1 or 2 percent reserve "venture fund," as Ed Roach terms it, to support new initiatives is also a potent means of encouraging change. The University of North Carolina at Asheville has employed this method effectively to fund designated program "thrust areas."

Among other control systems that bear importantly on the effective implementation of a strategic vision are the reward system, the information system, and the assessment system of an institution. The provision of enchanced program funding, for example, to reward progress can be a strong incentive for continued change. An institution's information system must be integrated to provide an overall picture of operations and an adequate data base for monitoring progress and trend changes.

Finally, regular scanning of the internal and external environments together with a frequent review of the results of efforts allow for ongoing revision of plans. Continuous revision is one of the distinguishing characteristics of strategic planning. As David Brown notes, a strategic vision is never finished, always evolving. A strategic approach is flexible. Rather than accomplishing straight-line progress, the institution that works strategically is more likely to "meander toward a dream," adapting goals and correcting course as circumstances nfold. Strategically run institutions employ not a fixed plan, but a planning cycle, whether it be as brief as two years, as at Carnegie Mellon, or as long as five years, as at West Texas State University.

The Benefits of Strategic Planning

Strategic planning offers many advantages. One of the greatest is a clarification of the mission and identity of a college or university that will, in turn, allow a focused deployment of resources. Centre College of Kentucky found important truths in its "central myth." By examining carefully what it means to be a small, selective, residential, coeducational college of the liberal arts, Centre defined a mission to become a model of national consequence for institutions of its character and opened possibilities for important improvement in its fortunes. The University of Louisville achieved increased stature as an urban institution, rooted in its community and charged with an enhanced research role. The University of Miami came forward as a leading independent comprehensive research university, with vastly augmented resources. Carnegie Mellon University focused its academic programs and departments in ways that buttressed its mission, which emphasizes research and technical education in partnership with liberal learning; in the process, it greatly strengthened its academic and material resources. The University of North Carolina at Asheville made striking gains in quality, while seizing on the opportunities contained in a strong undergraduate liberal arts tradition, expanded ties with its service area, and the creation of a campus master plan. West Texas State University successfully weathered state financial difficulties, improved its academic quality, achieved greater efficiency by reorganizing structurally and focusing its programs, and attracted important new support for program initiatives. Westminster College not only avoided bankruptcy but also attained unprecedented prosperity and academic reputation, as its plans evolved to reply to unfolding challenges.

That several of these institutions effectively countered enrollment problems emphasizes the close connection between the advent of strategic planning in higher education and the coming of the new era of competition for students. Strategic planning expresses the arrival of the age of marketing in academia. The quest for institutional uniqueness, for differentiation, for comparative advantage, for a "niche," is essentially the search for an advantageous market position. Strategic planning is fundamentally a means of applying marketing concepts to higher education.

The core of the marketing idea is the notion of matching production or service capabilities to demand. That is why environmental scanning is so important an element in strategic management, which seeks primarily to adapt an organization to changes that will affect its clientele. Institutions of higher education, however, are limited in one important aspect in their ability to apply the marketing concept. They are not capable of as broad a range of responses as are firms in the profit sector. Their mission, while it may be in part to survive (the equivalent of earning a profit in the profit sector), is more. It is at bottom to act, to make decisions as Edward Foote so aptly puts it, "in keeping with the fundamental principles of human learning." Hence, they must remember, in Foote's words, to resist "the danger of too much orientation toward shifting markets and too little toward the essence of what a university must continue to do, regardless of market forces." In the face of tension between mission and market forces, colleges and universities must maintain a precarious balance if they are to be true to their basic purposes. That is a principal reason why the contributors to this book have so often stressed doing well all that is undertaken.

The Limits of Strategic Planning

Institutions that look toward strategic planning must also recall that, as Donald Swain writes, "There are no panaceas in managing a major university [or a college]." Strategic planning is a useful tool, but it cannot solve all problems. It cannot, for example, guarantee capital or operating funds to an insolvent institution, although it might, if visionary and well conceived, attract critically needed students and support, as it did at Westminster. It cannot provide strength where there is none or quality when that is lacking.

It is also true that strategic planning faces formidable obstacles. One of these is sheer inertia—the fact that it is generally more comfortable to continue to act in habitual ways even when a crisis looms. Another is that, as Richard Cyert notes, strategic planning obliges one to deal with an ambiguous future, and many academicians are averse to ambiguity and risk and have chosen professorial careers for the security they offer. It is also the case that, as Clark Kerr has said, faculty do not like to plan and presidents are "not masochistic."

Sensitivity to a college's or a university's corporate culture, as well as to its decentralized decision-making apparatus, thus becomes critical. Successful strategic planning requires, all of our writers agree, presidential leadership of the highest order. Consultants may, at times, perform useful or even vital roles in inspiring plans. Presidents, however, must take the primary initiative. Perhaps nowhere as much as in the realm of strategic planning is the president's role as bard, soothsayer, seer, prophet, spinner of dreams, and exhorter to action so important. Nor, perhaps, anywhere else is the need for the president to use all available means in the decentralized academic institution to forge consensus so vital. The imperative to balance leadership with consent, illustrated repeatedly in these pages, is one of the most daunting of managerial balancing acts. Even at Westminster, which temporarily had to embrace secrecy in planning, success depended as much on winning faculty acceptance as it did on the vision and leadership of administrators. The need for faculty consent is the basis of the repeated observation that the form of change most likely to result from strategic leadership is evolutionary. Even evolutionary change will often be hard won, for any change brings losers as well as winners. Any change diminishes some programs and interests while enhancing others. And, midstream in a transition, there is always the possibility, if not the inevitability, of getting caught in what Ed Roach poignantly and pointedly calls the "valley of despair," when the costs of change are all too evident, the benefits not yet realized, and critics abound.

It is thus understandable that strategic planning is apt to win most ready acceptance where there are real and perceived external threats or opportunities. One can appreciate how and why a distinguished and prosperous institution, with remarkable strengths and self-assurance but little of the will for self-correction, can easily spurn the opportunities that a strategic approach might promise. One can understand how a professional school in deep trouble, whose own graduates derogate it but whose faculty remains smugly and narrowly self-satisfied, can reject a strategic option and continue to slide toward oblivion. Most of all, one can speculate not only that the resourcefulness and resiliency displayed by institutions embracing stategic planning are reassuring signs of vitality that hold high promise for the future but also that leadership in higher education will shift increasingly to institutions with the vision and the will to undertake strategic planning.

Reference

Carroll, L. *Through the Looking Glass*. New York: Crown Publishers, 1982. (Originally published 1872.)

Douglas W. Steeples is dean of the College of Liberal and Fine Arts at the University of Southern Colorado and has served as executive vice-president and academic dean at Westminster College, Utah.

Index

U.S. Postal Service

STATEMENT OF OWNERSHIP, MANAGEMENT AND CIRCULATION
Required by 39 U.S.C. 3685

1A. Title of Publication	1B. PUBLICATION NO.							2. Date of Filing
New Directions for Higher Education	9	9	0	–	8	8	0	10/26/88

3. Frequency of Issue	3A. No. of Issues Published Annually	3B. Annual Subscription Price
quarterly	4	$39 indiv./ $52 inst.

4. Complete Mailing Address of Known Office of Publication *(Street, City, County, State and ZIP+4 Code) (Not printers)*

350 Sansome Street, San Francisco, CA 94104

5. Complete Mailing Address of the Headquarters of General Business Offices of the Publisher *(Not printer)*

350 Sansome Street, San Francisco, CA 94104

6. Full Names and Complete Mailing Address of Publisher, Editor, and Managing Editor *(This item MUST NOT be blank)*
Publisher *(Name and Complete Mailing Address)*

Jossey-Bass Inc., Publishers, 350 Sansome Street, San Francisco, CA 94104

Editor *(Name and Complete Mailing Address)*

Martin Kramer, 2807 Shasta Rd., Berkeley, CA 94708

Managing Editor *(Name and Complete Mailing Address)*
Allen Jossey-Bass, Jossey-Bass Inc., Publishers
350 Sansome Street, San Francisco, CA 94104

7. Owner *(If owned by a corporation, its name and address must be stated and also immediately thereafter the names and addresses of stockholders owning or holding 1 percent or more of total amount of stock. If not owned by a corporation, the names and addresses of the individual owners must be given. If owned by a partnership or other unincorporated firm, its name and address, as well as that of each individual must be given. If the publication is published by a nonprofit organization, its name and address must be stated.) (Item must be completed.)*

Full Name	Complete Mailing Address
Jossey-Bass Inc., Publishers	350 Sansome Street San Francisco, CA 94104

For names and addresses of stockholders, see attached list

8. Known Bondholders, Mortgagees, and Other Security Holders Owning or Holding 1 Percent or More of Total Amount of Bonds, Mortgages or Other Securities *(If there are none, so state)*

Full Name	Complete Mailing Address
same as #7	

9. For Completion by Nonprofit Organizations Authorized To Mail at Special Rates *(DMM Section 423.12 only)*
The purpose, function, and nonprofit status of this organization and the exempt status for Federal income tax purposes *(Check one)*

(1) ☐ Has Not Changed During Preceding 12 Months	(2) ☐ Has Changed During Preceding 12 Months	*If changed, publisher must submit explanation of change with this statement.*

10. Extent and Nature of Circulation *(See instructions on reverse side)*	Average No. Copies Each Issue During Preceding 12 Months	Actual No. Copies of Single Issue Published Nearest to Filing Date
A. Total No. Copies *(Net Press Run)*	2000	2030
B. Paid and/or Requested Circulation 1. Sales through dealers and carriers, street vendors and counter sales	314	15
2. Mail Subscription *(Paid and/or requested)*	1005	1052
C. Total Paid and/or Requested Circulation *(Sum of 10B1 and 10B2)*	1319	1067
D. Free Distribution by Mail, Carrier or Other Means Samples, Complimentary, and Other Free Copies	103	210
E. Total Distribution *(Sum of C and D)*	1422	1277
F. Copies Not Distributed 1. Office use, left over, unaccounted, spoiled after printing	578	753
2. Return from News Agents		
G. TOTAL *(Sum of E, F1 and 2—should equal net press run shown in A)*	2000	2030

11. I certify that the statements made by me above are correct and complete	Signature and Title of Editor, Publisher, Business Manager, or Owner *[signature]* Vice-President

PS Form **3526**, Dec. 1987 · *(See instructions on reverse)*